OUR CULTURE OF GREED

# OUR CULTURE OF GREED
## *When is enough enough?*

by Robert Hinde

*St. John's College,
Cambridge*

SPOKESMAN

First published in 2015 by
Spokesman
Russell House, Bulwell Lane
Nottingham NG6 0BT
England
Phone 0115 9708318   Fax 0115 9420433
e-mail elfeuro@compuserve.com
www.spokesmanbooks.com

Copyright © Robert A. Hinde 2015

All rights reserved. Except for the quotation of short passages for the purposes of criticism and review, no part of this publication may be reproduced, stored in a retrieval system of transmitted in any form or by means, electronic, mechanical, photocopying, recording or otherwise, without prior permission of the publishers.

British Library Cataloguing in Publication Data
A CIP catalogue record for this book is available from the British Library

ISBN 978 0 85124 846 2

Printed in Nottingham by The Russell Press (www.russellpress.com)

*He that hath two coats, let him to impart to him that hath none; and he that hath meat, let him do likewise. Luke, 3: 11.*

*'... national and world happiness can only be built up on a basis of unselfish devotion to the cause of others.' Tony Benn, 1943.*

# CONTENTS

| | |
|---|---:|
| **Preface** | **10** |
| **PART I. OUR PROBLEMS** | **11** |
| **Chapter 1. Society Today** | **13** |
| **Chapter 2. Realistic Optimism** | **19** |

    Banish despair
    A broad perspective is needed
    Science and morality
    Dialectical relations between levels of social complexity
    Summary

| | |
|---|---:|
| **Part II. MORALITY** | **29** |
| **Chapter 3. What Is Morality?** | **31** |

    The development of psychological propensities
    The development of morality in individuals
    The evolution of morality
    Evolutionary sources of morality
        Threat of revenge
        Authority
        Religious morality
        Parental care and nepotism
        Reciprocity
        'Egalitarian' societies
        Inter-group conflict

| | |
|---|---:|
| **Chapter 4. Why Behave Morally?** | **47** |

    Independent origins of belief and morality
    Does religious belief have beneficial consequences
      for morality?
    The conscience
    Intuition or rational debate?
    Summary

**Part III. CHANGE IS NECESSARY**     **53**

**Chapter 5. Background for change**     **55**
    The task is not easy
    Goals must be limited
    Materialism
    Conflict is inevitable
    Blinkered views
    Is morality passé
    Is the time ripe?
    Summary

**Chapter 6. Towards a new morality**     **61**
    How we see the world
    Carrot and Stick
    An absolute or a flexible morality
    Criteria
    Religious morality
    Summary

**Part IV AREAS FOR CHANGE**     **71**

**Chapter 7. The marketplace**     **73**
    Competition
    Competition and capitalism
    Inequalities
    Poverty
    Taming business competition
    Employee ownership
    Summary

**Chapter 8: Some other institutions**     **85**
    Politics
    War
    Churches
    Summary

**Chapter 9: Personal and group relations**     **90**
    Population growth
    Urban living

    Personal relationships
    Education
    Human rights and responsibilities
    Individualism and collectivism
    Summary

## Part V. ADJUSTMENTS ARE POSSIBLE     103

## Chapter 10. We have the potential     105
    Introduction
    Cultural differences
    Concepts of fairness
    'Egalitarian' societies
    Some features of our own culture
    The example of Japan
    Changes in values in modern societies
    Inducing change in world-views
    Summary

## Chapter 11. Conclusion     120

## References     123

## Index     133

# Preface

A personal note may be in order. On retirement from a research career in biology and psychology, and a spell of administration, I put nearly all my energies into a) persuading people that war is not a sensible way to solve problems and b) trying to understand the nature of religion.

The former involved membership of the international *Pugwash Conferences on Science and World Affairs*, primarily concerned with providing accurate information to politicians, with the aim of abolishing nuclear weapons. I am also a member of the *Campaign for Nuclear Disarmament* and the *Movement for the Abolition of War*, trying to persuade the general public that war is not a sensible way to solve differences.

Trying to understand religion led me to see that the really important thing was how one *behaved*, not what one believed. That has led to a focus on morality. In the present volume I have drawn on what I have written before, which inevitably involves some repetition, but it marks a step forward in my quest. At 91, it is a swan song indicating where I have got to. Writing it has been a bit like lying down with a many-headed monster, with many jaws ready to snap. I am well aware that trying to synthesize aspects of many disciplines while at the same time trying to be brief has exposed me to many dangers, and it is improbable that I have avoided all of them.

I am indebted to many people, but most especially to Joan Stevenson-Hinde for discussions and help at all stages. The following were among the many colleagues and friends who have contributed comments and criticisms (but do not necessarily share the views expressed): Lara Adams, Carol Berman, Peter Clarke, John Cozens-Hardy, Partha Dasgupta, Duncan Dormor, John Finney, Kit Hill, Camilla Hinde, Kate McCullough, Joelien Pretorius, Pete Richerson, the late Joseph Rotblat, Thelma Rowell, Louise Shimizu, Tony Simpson, Simon Szreter, and Harvey Whitehouse.

# Part I
# Our Problems

## Chapter 1
# Society Today

On March 11th, 2011, a massive earthquake occurred near the coast of Japan. It was followed by a tsunami, a series of 30-foot high waves that devastated coastal areas, killed over 16,000 people and rendered countless homeless. And as if that wasn't enough, the tsunami damaged part of a nuclear power station, resulting in nuclear meltdown, release of nuclear materials into the environment and massive contamination of the ocean. To the surprise of many, little looting occurred in the aftermath of the disaster. Reports indicated that survivors, though desperate for food, still waited in line for groceries. In some of the devastated areas the survivors banded together and began to allocate the tasks necessary for their future joint survival – boiling water, scavenging for food and petrol, preparing food. Within at least some areas they established communities with impromptu governing bodies and communication with neighbouring refugee centres. A substantial number of students volunteered their time, spending months helping the disaster victims who were living in temporary shelters. The stoicism and self-sacrifice, the quiet bravery of the students in the face of tragedy, were remarkable to western reporters.

Yet such behaviour is certainly not unique. The same phenomenon is to be seen in many disaster situations the world over. For my generation the Blitz on London in the first years of World War II showed how external threat, the apparent imminence of defeat by a ruthless enemy, brought mutual aid to the fore. This was not only a case of helping others while the bombs were falling or dramatic rescues from burning buildings, but more importantly a pervasive feeling of 'we are all in this together'. 'Got a light, mate?' became a common form of address between members of the forces meeting in cold railway station buffets, or 'shift over, chum' in an overcrowded train.

Reports show that the same feeling was prominent in German cities under allied bombardment. The history of warfare provides countless examples on a smaller scale. There was a similar response to the destruction of the Twin Towers in New York City on September 11th 2001. It is as though disaster and the suffering of others can jolt complacency, changing the way in which people see the world from a focus primarily on their own interests to a realisation of the needs of the community in which they live.

But this is certainly not just a wartime phenomenon. Our societies could not exist without some feeling of mutuality; without recognition, perhaps unconscious, that our well-being depends on that of others, and theirs on ours. Many people do in fact consider others' welfare among their own personal concerns (Farsides, 2013; Frimer et al. 2011). Gentiles who exposed themselves to great danger by rescuing Jews from Nazi persecution regarded the intergroup differences between Jew and Gentile as without significance (Monroe, 2010). On an everyday level, only today my wife, struggling to get a trolley containing purchases from the supermarket to the car in a torrential downpour, was suddenly conscious of a stranger holding an umbrella half over her head and saying 'We can share this.' It is unnecessary to give further examples, one needs only to think about one's everyday life.

I emphasise the extent to which we feel part of a community, and the ways in which it may affect our behaviour, because we certainly do not always feel positively about our neighbours: many factors tend to cause us to mistrust them. The media's emphasis on murders, muggings, burglaries, kidnaps, scandals and petty crimes of various sorts carries the lesson: 'you cannot trust anybody these days'. The plots of many of the novels we read, and the films and plays that we see revolve around violence or deception. The books I read as a boy in the thirties involved overcoming either evil people by the hero ('Bulldog Drummond', who could 'shoot out a fist like a leg of mutton' or 'the Saint' who could throw a knife with deadly accuracy – always, like Robin Hood, in a good cause) or adverse circumstances (attempting to reach the South pole or climb Mount Everest). Today the circumstances are different but the themes are basically similar, usually involving goodies, who you hope will win, and baddies who must lose in the end. I am not forgetting the classics: the nineteenth century novelists, though with much more subtlety, and without violence, are there too. So we cannot blame it all on literature or the media: they are only feeding us with that for which we crave.

But pause to reflect for a moment. It is clear that today, unless you have been quite exceptionally unlucky, you received many more kind, helpful or positive responses than negative ones. Why do you notice them less? Is it just because kind or positive responses are more commonplace? Or is BAD somehow more salient than GOOD? We forget too easily the kindness shown by others but remember their cruelty, selfishness, thoughtlessness and egocentricity.

As a convenient approximation, we can describe our behaviour as involving two propensities: to behave 'prosocially' with kindness and consideration to others, cooperating with them when it furthers their interests (and perhaps one's own); and a propensity to behave with selfish assertiveness, including greed, assertiveness, aggression and so on. It hardly needs to be said that 'prosociality' and 'selfish assertiveness' is each a mere shorthand for a variety of types of behaviour: the two categories are both clearly heterogeneous, but they are useful for heuristic purposes. They cease to be useful if pressed too far, and I am making no claim that they involve entirely separate mechanisms. Indeed, excessive kindness can be counter-productive and lead to rejection by the recipient, who may perceive it as a product of selfish assertiveness. However the two labels, if used with caution, are useful for heuristic purposes. *In general, moral behaviour is that in which prosociality predominates.*

As another metaphor, we see the world through alternative spectacles – as populated by selfish greedy individuals with whom we must be circumspect, or by our friends, whom we know we can trust and we know will be kind, generous and considerate. And it is how we see the world, our world-view, that affects the balance between selfish assertiveness and prosociality.

Today, selfish assertiveness in other people's behaviour seems much more salient than prosociality. The gap between the haves and the have nots is already much too wide and getting wider: in the United Kingdom the wealthier citizens have assets hundreds of times greater than those of the least wealthy (Piketty, 2012). Many couples with young children cannot afford the mortgage deposit on a home. Although crime in general may be decreasing, the abuse of alcohol and drugs is widespread, especially amongst young people who are provided with inadequate outlets for their energy. Although governmental corruption is said to be higher in 'poor' nations than in 'rich' ones (World Bank, 2005), in many so-called democratic countries powerful lobbies from unelected sources distort governmental policies away from the interests of the voters. Some politicians have been shown to lie and fiddle their expenses.

As things are, the rich can avoid the debts they owe to society by pretending to live in tax havens. Those who manipulate the financial markets can get many times the income of those who make a positive contribution to society: a successful financier can 'earn' tens of millions of pounds in a single year while contributing virtually nothing to society. We have allowed ourselves to be drawn into a celebrity culture, where entrepreneurs can receive vast sums by exploiting a young woman who has been born with a pretty face. We have devised institutions to serve ourselves and are finding that they encourage greed and status-seeking to spread like a cancer through society (chapters 7 & 8). Morality has been forced into a back seat. A century after the war to end wars lives are still being ruined by war. The consequences of natural disasters, drought, floods, forest fires, earthquakes, tsunamis cannot be adequately ameliorated because emergency services are inadequate. They are inadequate because we are insufficiently concerned with our neighbours: what happens elsewhere is of too little concern to us. That is not to underestimate the devoted work of the non-governmental organisations (NGOs): OXFAM, Médecins Sans Frontières, UN Agencies and many others do vital work, but their resources are always limited. Even the aid promised by the affluent countries is inadequate, tardy and diluted by fingers that pick away at the pot before it gets to where it is needed.

No doubt the causal bases for our malaise are multiple, but they include the growth of individualistic capitalism and the increasing wealth gap, as well as the increase in the scale of society. With the dispersal of kin, 'neighbours' are often strangers, and personal relationships are downplayed. The disruptive forces in society, and the results of human egoism multiplied by the powers of technological, commercial and governmental domination, are becoming too powerful for community impulses to cope with. Moral systems face special challenges today from the growth of technology. Sometimes, as with genetic engineering, the moral implications of new technologies are not immediately apparent. Sometimes, as with environmental issues and global warming, the moral implications are clear but run counter to the individual interests of many of those involved in controlling the technologies in question (Dasgupta 2001). So I am not saying that people are less 'moral' than they used to be in any absolute sense, but that the morality to which many subscribe may not be adequate for the modern world. And the problems do not come only from those at the top: the phone hacking journalists may be obeying their masters, but their intrusions into the private lives of politicians and celebrities are made to satisfy an apparently insatiable public demand for dirt.

How do the greedy ones get away with it? A society of greedy people is certainly not one in which most people would want to live, yet the greed that leads to a grossly unfair distribution of society's resources is too often accepted. Do the stories of the filthy rich provide us with entertainment? Do they grab our imaginations, enabling us to live imaginary lives of abundance and narcissism by projecting ourselves into the roles of the rich? More generally, are we too ready to see assertive self-interest as a GOOD? We admire and envy the very rich and successful, and the very rich see nothing wrong in their riches, ignoring those they have trampled on.

The rot is widespread, but it need not be so. At first sight the obvious remedies lie in finding better political, economic or financial systems. We try to fiddle with our present society, to create a capitalism more concerned with the public interest (Sainsbury, 2013). However that will never be enough: the remedies will be aimed at curtailing the activities of the greedier individuals. The assumption of the politicians, economists and financiers is usually that selfish assertiveness must be kept within limits while little attention is paid to encouraging prosociality.

Both the two propensities, prosociality and selfish assertiveness, are essential, but a balance between them must be found if the society is to persist. If selfish assertiveness predominated in most individuals, the society would disintegrate. If all individuals were predominantly prosocial, caring only for the welfare of others, the society would be vulnerable to selfish free-riders and soon lose its character. Those individuals who look after their own interests seem to do better, other things being equal, than those who are merely passive. But humans have always lived in groups: group-living gave our hunter/gatherer ancestors better protection from outside dangers, whether from marauding individuals, rival groups, or physical calamities, and enabled them to hunt more efficiently. Group living requires some consideration for our peers.

The two propensities, to act prosocially and to act selfishly, are inevitably in conflict within families, groups and societies. Unless concern with one's own outcomes were controlled this could lead to the loss of the advantages of group-living. Concerns with one's own welfare, even one's own petty desires, get in the way of prosocial concern for others. Selfish assertiveness is to the individual actor's benefit and usually seems to predominate, but a consequence of acting morally is to reduce ill-feeling and conflict in the group, making cooperation and positive relationships between individuals possible (Irons, 1991). It has been shown in a variety of animal species that positive relationships between individuals are associated with less stress, greater infant survival, and longer life (Seyfarth & Cheney,

2012; cf. Alexander, 1979). A basic theme of this book is that the function of morality is to limit conflict in humans. Most obviously it acts to limit selfish assertiveness, but on occasion it may limit prosociality to produce a balance. Conventions as to what is proper behaviour pervade our outlook on the world and are adapted by the society and maintained by social pressure. Some aspects of morality are reified as laws and maintained by punishment for defectors, though force can be misused by authorities in hierarchical regimes.

Amending political, economic or financial systems will never be enough. With society as it is, there will always be some who find weak spots in new regulations. Amended laws will be drafted, but they will merely give greedy individuals new chances to find new loopholes to exploit. Changing the Government will not be adequate unless we also give greater priority to our morality. We need to dig deeper, to look at the inadequacy of the principles that underpin policies and pervade the lives of nearly every individual in our society. This means changing the spectacles with which we see society. Aristotle's conclusion that a good life must include the good of the larger society in which we live has become drowned by the greed and status-seeking which play too large a part in our lives and infect the way in which we see the world. Only when we put exclusive self-interest away in its proper place will we be able to move forward. At the moment we see morality as outside ourselves, as controls on what we do. We must move towards a society in which our moral guidelines become part of ourselves.

In this book I argue that we could do better. The bases of most of our problems lie in the way in which we see the world, manifested in the greed and status-seeking that seem so often to characterise the behaviour of *other people*. They seem just to want more than their share. But humans are not just self-seeking: there is this different side to our natures that is struggling for expression. Mistakenly, in seeking for false goals, we have built a society where competitiveness rules, where too many of us are striving too hard to do down our neighbours. We forget the pleasures of living at peace, in harmony with our neighbours. We forget in part because it can seem impossible to get out of the morass we have got ourselves into. But the concluding chapters discuss some of the facets of our nature that, if allowed expression, could allow us to build more harmonious societies. We do not have to live like this.

Chapter 2

# Realistic Optimism

**Banish despair**
The first obstacle to be overcome is despair. It is too easy to regard the social problems of our society as insoluble, to turn our backs on them and get on with something else. This may be especially the case in the middle class society in which I live. Many of my academic colleagues regard efforts to promote a world without violence, and especially one without nuclear weapons, with tolerant disdain. War has always been with us, they say, and always will be: the genie of nuclear weapons cannot be put back in the bottle. Others say that our moral judgements are part of human nature, and cannot be changed. Of course, if everyone thought like that they would be right, but I shall try to convince you that they are wrong.

More importantly, we have the potential to build a better world, though it will take a little time and require a great deal of determination. As noted already, while the media report crimes and disasters, that is not even half the picture: the media seldom report acts of kindness, generosity or self-sacrifice although, and perhaps because, most of us receive and make many prosocial actions every day: that we do so is not 'news'. The tsunami in Japan was described and portrayed in detail in the media, but too little attention was given to the prosocial behaviour it elicited in survivors and rescue workers, or to those who continue to attempt to control the nuclear pollution at great personal risk years later. We must recognise this bias. It is easy to talk about greed and selfishness, but difficult to talk about moral behaviour. Yet it is a fact that people can be kind, help those in trouble, look after the handicapped, and may sacrifice themselves for the sake of the community. Surely a little more emphasis on that side of human nature is essential if we are to solve our problems? I am not suggesting that it is possible or likely (or even perhaps desirable) that we could have a society of completely prosocial individuals, but the need at the moment is a little more emphasis on the positive side of human nature.

Unfortunately this is dangerous ground, for it has become unfashionable to talk about morality, and especially for a scientist to do so: it is seen as inevitably ethnocentric and imprecise, mushy, and inviting scorn. Never mind, it is undeniable that greed and excessive self-interest are central to our problems and we must confront the facts:

to make progress towards a better society we need a slight change in our world-view.

In some countries there are signs of improvement, at least in some areas. Pockets of slavery and the trafficking of women still exist in some places, including the UK, but major steps towards elimination of the slave trade bore fruit nearly two centuries ago. Wars still break out, but it is increasingly seen that war is not only nearly always immoral but also a foolish way to try to settle disputes. Violence breeds violence, but in Europe at least war is seen by most people as a method of last resort for settling international differences.

This change has been related to an increase in the positive value placed on human life: most western countries have abolished capital punishment, several States in the USA being regrettable exceptions. Again, while far too many live in poverty, at least society does not simply accept it and real efforts are made to raise public awareness of the problem and to alleviate and abolish poverty. So we must take courage from the fact that some improvement is occurring, at least in some contexts in the West, and do what we can to hasten the process. We must not sit back and leave it to others. The eighth deadly sin is resignation and hopelessness.

**A broad perspective is needed**
Greed and status-seeking sometimes seem to be ubiquitous. Where morality or its absence is the issue, many turn to religion. It has after all been the principal purveyor of our morality over the centuries. The morality that religions have espoused has, on the whole, withstood the tests of time, but the incidence of greed in our society leads one to suppose that the churches are not making a very good job of ensuring that morality remains a force in people's lives. It is undeniable that greed and self-interest are central to our problems and we must confront the facts: to make progress towards a better society we need to understand the bases of morality.

I certainly do not want to imply that I think I have a cure for all our ills. But I do believe that no cure will be found unless we make use of all the sources of knowledge that are available to us, take a cross-disciplinary approach and work at several levels simultaneously. Although things are improving, psychology, social psychology, sociology, physical anthropology, social anthropology, history, ethology and studies of evolution still tend to proceed in isolation, though the problems that confront them need input from a variety of sources. And, for understanding morality, we need an approach that includes an especially broad perspective.

It has often been claimed that science can have nothing to say about morality. It is argued that morality deals with unquantifiable subjective phenomena and 'spiritual' matters while science deals with facts about what is, not with how they ought to be. I contest that view. Our model should be not, or not only, the physical sciences, but the behavioural and social sciences that deal with the complex phenomena that result from the behaviour of intentional beings and their interactions. Subjective phenomena, such as fear, wonder or guilt, are part of our lives and are becoming the immediate focus for many studies. They are essential as intervening variables to explain overt behaviour. They have a role directly comparable with those of the gene in biology and the electric current in physics as first proposed: they refer to postulated entities useful at least initially to explain observed phenomena but whose physical nature may or may not be revealed by subsequent study. It is indeed the case that the study of morality must concern itself with phenomena that appear to be unique, non-repeatable and non-quantifiable, but such problems are common also for the social scientist and neuropsychologist.

Realising that, we must re-consider our morality as only the start. Consideration of the nature of our morality, of how we have come to hold the values we hold rather than any others, will help us to prioritise our goals. Except perhaps for a few at the top of our hierarchical societies, most of us would prefer a more equitable society, with power shared more evenly or at least more appropriately amongst individuals. We would prefer it because it would be 'more fair', but also because it would enable us to live without many (though unfortunately perhaps not all) of the tensions prevalent in current societies. The behavioural propensities that could make more satisfying societies possible are present in every one of us, but are no longer given the priority they deserve. I shall argue that that can change if we order our values and our world-view appropriately.

But it is not only a matter of ordering our priorities, we must recognise our prosocial potentials. Humans may be inherently selfish, but they are also inherently prosocial. At some level, we all want to help our fellows, we do not want a society where dog bites dog is the sole order of the day. That means diluting the desire to do the best for oneself and aiming also to enhance the common well-being. Of course that raises a host of problems. Just because individuals differ, you cannot please everyone and too many pates have been bloodied in disputes over what is best for all (Hollenbach, 2002). I shall leave that on one side with the reminder of how mutual aid becomes more salient when communities face disaster (pp. 13-14), though I question whether disasters are necessary for our prosocial propensities to be revealed.

**Science and morality**
Some will think that an approach that starts with morality is an inappropriate course for a scientist to take: there have been countless attempts to make the world a better place by influencing how people behave and what they value, and most have been by philosophers or theologians. You may well ask whether a scientist has the right tools to intrude on this field (Bateson, 1989)? Philosophers who claim that science is concerned solely with what people do, and not with what they ought to do, are in my view out of date. Subjective judgements of right and wrong are made in the brain, and in the end it will be the scientist's business to understand them. Anyway, philosophers, it seems, are not wholly satisfied with the progress made in moral philosophy (Williams, 1985); politicians, with their eyes on the electorate, are too inclined to seek short-term solutions; economists have been inclined to assume that all humans are simply greedy; legislators tend to wake up only when change is overdue. Perhaps it will help if we can gain a little understanding of the bases of our morality, and the relations of our morality to how we actually behave. But for that natural science must be married to the humanities and, I am not ashamed to admit, to common sense.

You may be scornful of attempts to make the world a better place. You may say humans are inevitably greedy and self-seeking. OK, so let us examine where that greed comes from, what makes some people greedier than others. Scientists will say that our differences from each other are due to interaction between our genes and our experiences as we develop from the womb through infancy and childhood into adolescence and adulthood. Nobody can disagree with that, though we are still way off understanding all the details. But what determines the differences in experience between people brought up in Tokyo, London and Jerusalem? It is easy to answer glibly 'differences in culture'. What does that mean? Mostly it means differences in the accepted ways people interact with each other and the values they hold. If we want to improve the world we must change our culture – not replace it in major ways, but nudge it a little so that we have a more harmonious world.

That means some change for each one of us, not just in those at the top. Many of you will say that sounds like preaching: it is what the priests have been saying for millennia. In general yes, but with differences in important detail.

For the sake of fellow scientists, I must make two reservations here. First, good science requires measurement and the testing of hypotheses. Many scientists would regard my fumbling in the darkness of ignorance as mushy hand-waving. They would say that my science is diluted with too much common sense, and we all know how misleading common sense can be. To that I would say that the problem of society's malaise is of such immeasurable importance that a new attempt must be made. Second, I feel that the need at the moment is for a brief synthetic approach. That may be dangerous, because in attempting to be brief one inevitably skates over distinctions and problems of profound importance: my only excuse is that I have tried to keep my eye on the ball. Of course I have been led into areas in which I am not expert; of course a focus on morality and our world-view will not be adequate by itself, but the bottom-up approach that I advocate may help us to inculcate the values and build the political, financial and legal systems that we need for more stable, peaceful and wholesome societies. At least we can make a start. I am not claiming to present a morality that will suit everyone all the time in every situation, in fact I believe that such a code may be impossible to attain. And of course I do not claim that we can turn the world or even our culture around in a year or two: we need a new view of the world, and we do not yet know exactly what form it should take. But we do have some idea.

And, I would say, let those who laugh at the naiveté of the idea that fiddling with morality will help us have their laugh: when I was a young academic I was teased by five historians in my college who thought that the idea that an ornithologist (as I then was) could do any good was hilarious – 'We historians, we know that nothing will put the world to rights'. Such cynicism will get us nowhere, and fortunately not all historians are like that. And I fully acknowledge that it is impossible to write about the world's ills without being hypocritical, but in striving for a better world one must disregard one's own shortcomings.

I shall argue that our moral values are not just givens, but part of the world we live in because we create them as we go along. We must live with the contradiction between the near-necessity of regarding our moral values as absolute, and knowing that they must change with time and circumstance. We have to come to terms with the mutual influences between what we do and what we value on the one hand, and the values of our culture and the political and economic systems we have developed on the other. But as a first step we need to understand our values and where they come from.

Of course we do not yet understand sufficiently well the immensely complex interplay between the biological, ecological, cultural and historical forces operating to be able to prescribe for particular situations. The discussion in this book is concerned with the general principles underlying moral codes, but an approach which draws on the natural and social sciences and on the humanities, and which indicates that moral systems must be based both in 'human nature' (p. 34) (its 'good' aspects but taking into account also its 'bad' ones) and in the society's history and current situation, and must change to meet new situations, does at least provide a starting point, and perhaps the only possible starting point. From there we can see which aspects of our behaviour and values most need our attention. It will be possible for us to achieve a better world because, as I shall show, the means are within our nature. Humans are too easily written off as just self-seeking: in reality we have the psychological characteristics that could lead to fairer, more equitable and more satisfying societies.

### Dialectical relations between levels of social complexity
Most people assume that the way to improve our present situation is to fiddle with the political, financial or economic systems. 'Things would be better with a Labour/Conservative or Democrat/Republican Government'. That is a top/down approach. We must work also from the bottom upwards. The attitudes and values of individuals are affected by the work of the politicians and economists, but reciprocally the attitudes and values of individuals affect those politicians and economists, and not only through the ballot box. Thus we must come to terms with the mutual influences between levels of social complexity (Fig 1).

Each level of social complexity has emergent properties not relevant to the level below. For example, although relationships are built upon antecedent behavioural interactions, relationships are more than a simple sum of interactions and have additional properties such as warmth, sensitivity, mutual understanding and so forth (Hinde, 1997).

Furthermore, we must come to terms with the complexities inherent in every group. We seldom, or perhaps never, act alone without influence from others, and only rarely can we act without affecting others. We even see ourselves in a different light when alone, when in

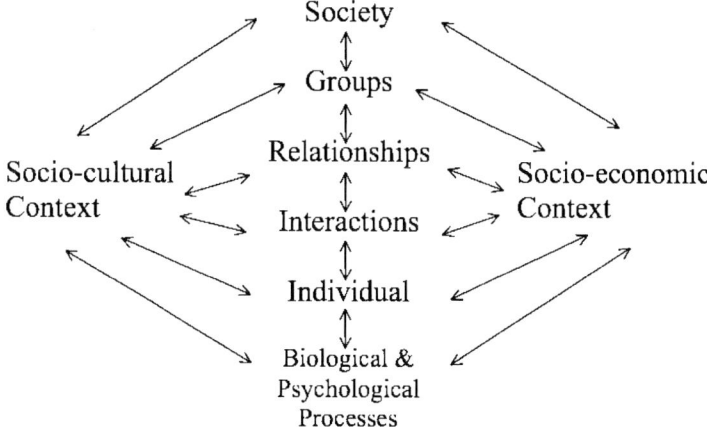

**Figure 1.** Framework indicating some of the dialectical relations between successive levels of social complexity.

our family, with colleagues or with strangers (e.g. Backman, 1988). Our attitude to everything in our environment may be influenced, one way or the other, by the attitudes and values of the group in which we live. Reciprocally, the group's attitudes and values result from those of the individuals that constitute the group, and the interactions between them. Similar effects operate throughout the successive levels of social complexity shown in Figure 1. How each individual behaves and what he/she values is affected (though not determined) by the world-views including the value structures of other group members, and how each individual behaves and what he/she values affects the behaviour and values of other members.

Two-way influences operate at every level and between levels of social complexity. For instance, how two individuals behave when they meet is influenced by their personalities. If they interact on successive occasions and form a relationship, the nature of that relationship is affected by their past interactions and in turn affects future ones. It may also affect their personalities. Similar two-way effects, though with differing mechanisms, operate between relationships and groups, and between groups and societies, as illustrated in Figure 1. Furthermore, every level affects and is affected by the socio-cultural and socio-economic structure (for instance, the world-views of individuals in the society, derived from its history, religion, social conventions and so on) and similarly for the relevant physical environment.

> *I shall use a concept 'world-view' that overlaps with a variety of concepts such as Public opinion, Zeitgeist, Weltanschauung, and so on, current in the social sciences, none of which have hard edges but which are essential for dealing with the complex phenomena of social organisation. I do not intend to discuss these concepts here, but shall use 'world-view' to refer to the aggregate of the attitudes, beliefs and values of an individual or group.*

The causal relations illustrated in Figure 1 are dialectical in that A affects and changes B; the changed B may then affect and change A; and the changed A may then affect and change the new B; who may then further affect the changed A and so on. Such effects must be considered also when an individual, a group, a convention, moral rule or value is involved: conventions affect how individuals behave, and how individuals behave and what they value affects the nature of the group's conventions and values. In general, this is the usual way in which values change: often it is what people do or say that changes first (perhaps as a consequence of changes in what they experience) and that affects other people's values, but sometimes a charismatic leader can change a group's values. In either case the dialectic operates (see Chapters 10-11).

Thus each individual, family, group and so on must be seen not as an isolated static entity but as in continuous processes of creation, maintenance or degradation through the dialectical influences with others. A consequence of all this is that any attempt to bring about social change is more likely to be successful if aimed both at the leaders and at the individuals in the street (see Figure 1). Some have claimed that aiming for the 'general good' may be an unachievable goal (Fehr & Fischbacker, 2003), but it is a respectable aim.

As an example of these dialectical influences, consider attitudes to divorce. Before World War II in most western countries, divorce was barely respectable: both moral attitudes and legal obstacles had to be overcome, and divorced individuals were regarded with reservation. In the UK the prejudice was so strong that it caused a King to abdicate. But during the war many couples were separated from each other, many men and women joined the Forces or went out to work, and in both cases were introduced to new ways of living. For that and other reasons, after the war many husbands and wives had drifted apart, and divorce became more frequent. As it became more frequent it became less disreputable, and as it became less disreputable it became more frequent. The ramifications of the resulting changes in societal values were immense.

This is important to the present issue: governments must recognise that putting penalties on greedy behaviour, or telling people not to be greedy, is unlikely to be effective for long. Some greedy people will be only partially affected and they will still get nearly all they can want, maybe a little more and maybe a little less than before, and they are likely to find other ways of satisfying their desires. The germ of greed will not be eradicated.

The speed with which changes in the socio-cultural structure in general, and in morality in particular, occur is highly variable. For the most part it is so slow we hardly notice it. I chose attitudes to divorce as an example because it has been encompassed in my lifetime, but I could equally well have chosen smoking, where change in public attitudes followed rapidly the publication of its effects on lung cancer, or the wearing of car seat-belts, where legislation was soon seen as sensible by most individuals. I experienced a sudden change in world-view in my first night on a troopship. We had previously been billeted in what had formerly been high quality flats in St. John's Wood, London. We were in small groups with shared toilets and bathroom. There was a happy feeling of 'We're all in this together' and will soon be qualified pilots. We then embarked on a cargo ship whose normal function was to bring meat from Argentine to Britain, but served as a troop ship on its outward journey. On the ship we slept in hammocks slung almost touching each other on large decks holding a hundred or more airmen. There was little in the way of comradeship: if one left anything for a moment, it was swiped. Those who had been comrades became rivals: one's world-view changed. I do not know how this arose, but I am sure the extreme crowding had something to do with it.

## Summary
1. Many, perhaps most, people are not satisfied with their lot. To make progress towards a better society, a multi-disciplinary approach is essential and we must take into account the full complexity of social life.
2. People can be incredibly kind, considerate and cooperative with each other, yet at other times people seem guided solely by selfishness.
3. As a first step in trying to ameliorate society's problems, it is useful

to see human behaviour as guided by two propensities, to be prosocial and to be selfishly assertive. (This is, of course, only a heuristic device, and carries no implications about mechanism.) At every level from the Government to the citizen, self-interest seems to guide decisions too often.
4. We look for solutions to our troubles by adjusting financial, economic or parliamentary systems, but the root causes are greed and self-advancement at all levels of social complexity. No measure will be fully successful unless the balance in decision-making between self-interest and the wellbeing of others is shifted slightly towards the latter.
5. We must ask whether our traditional moral values are fully adequate for the modern world, and how citizens can be persuaded to pay them more respect. That requires a multi-disciplinary approach.
6. This book argues for a change in world-view, and summarises evidence that change is possible.

# Part II
# **Morality**

Chapter 3

# What Is Morality?

In the last chapter I suggested that a basic cause of many of our troubles is 'greed', which is generally seen as a symptom of a lack of morality. I could add 'self-advancement' and other characteristics associated with it. Greed is defined as 'inordinate or insatiate longing, esp. for wealth' (Oxford English Dictionary). It is also usually seen as an inordinate desire to acquire or possess more than one needs, especially with respect to material wealth. In medieval Christianity, and in Dante's Divine Comedy, greed (*Avaritia*) was seen as one of the Seven Deadly Sins, but all the deadly sins involve an underlying focus on one's own needs or desires rather than those of other members of the community – lust, gluttony, greed, sloth, wrath, envy and pride. Nowadays condemnation of a desire to possess more than one needs is becoming salient through the effects of human activities on climate change. It plays a major role in the creation and maintenance of the growing gap between the circumstances of the rich and the poor in many societies (pp. 78-80).

However, seeing 'greed' as a 'desire' or 'longing' is no more than a description, and helps little in explanation. For that we need to ask at least two further questions: How has the propensity to be greedy evolved in our species, and how does it develop in each individual? Until recently it was quite usual to see the sources of greed to be related to a lack of religion. Religion, however, often seen as a unitary entity, is better seen as consisting of a number of components (Hinde, 2004a), the relations between them posing further questions (McKay & Whitehouse, 2014). In the case of the Abrahamic religions, one can recognise distinct components of belief, myths, ritual, morality, religious experience and the social concomitants. In the great majority of cases, the apparent unity of the several components of a religious system depends on the activities of religious specialists (priests and others) who use the supposed all-powerful nature of the god or gods to support moral rules and ritual that they see as in the society's best interests (and perhaps their own).

(The following will be familiar ground to many who see human physical and psychological characteristics as having evolved by variation and selection, natural and cultural. They should skip to page 34).

### The development of psychological propensities

Until the 1950s, the development of individual characteristics was generally seen as involving two processes, 'instinct' and 'learning'. Now we know that such a dichotomy (like, indeed, most dichotomies in this area) is too simple. The development of individuals, and of their physical and psychological properties, depends on continuing two-way influences between the organism as it is at each moment in time and the social/environmental factors to which it is exposed. Morality, which depends on a balance between prosociality and selfish assertiveness, must thus stem ultimately from 'human nature' which, as we shall see, has been shaped by natural and cultural selection in continuing interaction with the physical, biological and social environments that humans have experienced in evolutionary and historical time and that are experienced in the lifetime of each individual (Bateson & Gluckman, 2011). It is thus convenient to describe the individual as having a potential or propensity to develop the characteristic in question but requiring a particular experience or range of experiences to do so (Hinde, 2002). The experiences that are necessary are likely to change with development.

Let us briefly consider an example that played an important part in promoting this way of thinking. To give a slightly simplified account of the research, the chaffinch, a small perching bird, has a song that, though somewhat individually variable, is characteristic of the species. Individual males, reared without opportunity to hear chaffinch song, sing only a simple sequence of notes, but if exposed to chaffinch song in their first spring can learn to produce a normal chaffinch song. However, if exposed to the song of another species, they do not acquire it. In other words, they have a propensity to acquire chaffinch song if exposed to it, but no ability to learn the song of another species (Thorpe, 1961). In the same way, we learn some things more readily than others (Hinde & Stevenson-Hinde, 1973; Seligman & Hager, 1972). The old distinction between instinct and learning no longer has explanatory value.

An everyday example is the skin colour of white-skinned people, which darkens on exposure to sun. We could describe this by saying that we have a propensity to darken on exposure to sunlight. In Europeans white skin may be retained over a number of generations in the absence of adequate exposure to sunlight, while the propensity to darken with exposure to the sun is retained.

I shall use this simple model in discussing morality: we have propensities to behave prosocially and also to behave with selfish assertiveness, and which we do at any time depends in part on our experiences, past and current. The precise nature of the interaction between these propensities is complex and still only partially understood (see pp. 44-45): but if the experiential factors necessary for each propensity to be realised do not materialise, the propensity may still be carried on to the next generation or through many generations, until such time as the necessary experiential factors do appear.

**The development of morality in individuals**
The development of morality depends on the prior development of selfish assertiveness and prosociality, and there is growing evidence that both can appear quite early in a child's life. Every parent is aware that young children can behave assertively almost as soon as they are born: it is an important element in establishing a dialogue between mother and child.

The appearance of prosociality is less obvious, but a number of studies have shown that children may act prosocially in the second year of life (Warneken & Tomasello, 2009). However, at this age the child's prosocial behaviour depends on clues from the individual needing assistance that help is needed. Children aged two years or older will behave prosocially spontaneously even when the individual needing help gives no indication that help is needed – for instance dropping an object without appearing to notice. The children can then infer that an individual needs help even when the individual they help did not ask for help and was not aware that he needed it (Warneken, 2013).

**The evolution of morality**
How did morality evolve? As a biologist, I accept that evolutionary changes in morality from relatively simple origins to modern complexity has depended on variations in its several components, with the selection of some variants over others. In the example of the development of dark skin cited above, in some groups who live (or have lived) in sunny climates natural selection has apparently acted through the advantage of dark skin in sunny climates so that dark skin develops without the need for exposure to sunlight. By contrast, in Europeans white skin may be retained over a number of generations in the absence of adequate exposure to sunlight, while the propensity to darken with exposure to the sun is retained. This admittedly simplified account says nothing about the physiological processes involved. I should add here

that the details of how and why the particular characteristics of morality evolved in each society are as yet poorly understood, and depend on speculations on their apparent usefulness in the circumstances of that society. However, it is reasonable to suppose that it must involve the strength of the two propensities for prosociality and selfish assertiveness, and the balance between them.

Most discussion of evolutionary changes in physical characters in animals has implied that the bases of variation and selection lie in the relations between the genetic constitution of the individual and its experiences in the physical and social world. Variation in morality depends primarily on variation in the past and current social experiences of individuals. Furthermore, while in animals selection depends on differences in the variants' abilities to survive and/or reproduce, in the evolution of morality and many other aspects of culture the variants selected may be influenced by individual survival and reproduction only very indirectly (Dawkins, 1976). While animal evolution mostly involves the selection of some individuals' genes over others, in the human case the important variation may be between characters (e.g. particular moral conventions), or individuals or groups with different ways of behaving. How group selection works has been a matter of considerable controversy that would take us outside the theme of this book (Boyd & Richerson, 2005).

Propensities to develop a given character change relatively slowly over evolutionary time. It is therefore reasonable to suppose that aspects of morality that are common to all, or at least most, cultures are independent of differences between the cultural environments in which they develop. In other words, such aspects of morality are stable characters. The Golden Rule of do-as-you-would-be-done-by, or some variant thereof, is virtually pancultural. By contrast, aspects of morality that are peculiar to one or a few cultures are due to interaction between a propensity to develop the aspect of morality in question and aspects peculiar to the local social situations. But why have some characteristics of morality been selected and not others? In other words, what good does it do us to be moral?

**Evolutionary sources of morality**
We have seen that, by living in groups, our ancestors gained some protection from predators and rivals, but the proximity of peers must have led to competition for resources, including food and mates. Our ape ancestors, the common chimpanzee, the pygmy chimpanzee, and

more remotely the gorilla, both show a mixture of prosocial and aggressive behaviour to other members of the group or community in which they live (De Waal, 1996; Harcourt & Stewart, 2007; Wrangham et al., 2006). Some degree of conflict, overt or covert, is an inevitable consequence of group-living and thus changes in individual behaviour are necessary to make proximity acceptable. There, I suggest, lie the origins of morality: the selfish assertiveness of individuals must be attenuated to preserve the beneficial consequences of group living. Successful group living requires a balance between the two propensities, selfish assertiveness and prosociality.

If we are to understand morality as a product of evolution we must specify the benefits that each of these propensities confers. In the case of selfish assertiveness, the benefits are obvious: by behaving assertively, you get what you need or want. But the evolution of prosociality is more complicated, for a number of beneficial consequences have provided a basis for its selection. These have been regarded as stages in the evolution of prosociality (Alexander, 1979, 1987), but can better be seen as operating together.

*Threat of revenge*
At an early stage of human moral development, the one means for keeping selfishness in check was revenge. The fear of revenge if you did certain things served to establish what was permissible and what was not. Daly and Wilson (1988) examined the Human Relations Area Files, which summarise studies on many societies. They found evidence for the incidence of blood feuds in fifty-seven out of sixty cultures examined. Fear of revenge has been a major method of social control even in parts of Europe until quite recently, and a desire for revenge after being wronged is still common in our own societies (McCullough, 2008), though the oft-quoted Biblical stipulation that reparation should be in the same currency – 'an eye for an eye…' (Exodus, 21:24) – has been softened to 'equivalent value'. The power of the desire for revenge amongst the relatives of murder or rape victims in our own society is reported endlessly in the media. The threat of revenge, however, is not an entirely satisfactory method for maintaining good relations in a group, because individuals tend to see the harm done to them or their relatives as greater than that which they have done to others. Also their relatives are likely to help them take revenge, and the situation escalates. That can lead to violence or war, or to continuing tension that may last for generations (Evans-Pritchard, 1940, 1951).

Of course, forgiveness is possible, but it is difficult to achieve. McCullough (2008) argues that three conditions make it more probable: if the wronged party cares for the perpetrator of the injury, or values the relationship with him, or feels safe from him, forgiveness is more possible. The Truth and Reconciliation Commissions held in South Africa (Krog, 1999), and comparable proceedings elsewhere, confirm that injured parties can forgive even after the most horrific crimes (though they fall far short of justifying McCullough's postulation of a 'forgiveness instinct').

One can speculate that the possibility of revenge was a source of a sense of what one should not do. It would soon become apparent that if you did this or that, there would be trouble.

*Authority*
Continuing escalation in the reciprocation of revenge can be avoided if punishments for offending are administered not by the injured party but by an impartial authority. A history of Anglo-Saxon law (Adams, 1876) records that offences initially seen as offences against an individual or against the community came to be seen as offences against the 'King's Peace'. What had been 'folk peace' became the 'King's peace' and the authority for retribution became transferred from the wronged party to the community and later to the King. This had a second consequence. Early on outlawry was seen as the appropriate punishment for almost any offence, but later many offences were recognised as minor and could be expiated by a payment. Later part of the payment went to the injured party and part to the state or king as reparation for breaking the 'King's peace'.

*Religious morality*
Another potent source of moral values has been religious specialists. As each religious system became reasonably firmly established, some individuals became religious specialists – leaders, priests, rabbis, shamans or holders of one or the other roles in the system. Virtually every known human group contains specialists whose position in the society depends on their success in promoting the beliefs, rituals and customs of the society. They may then be regarded as more 'holy' than others. It is in their interests to purvey belief in deities with exceptional powers who promulgate moral values, and then to threaten people with divine punishment if they do not comply or to promise rewards if they do. This puts them in positions from which they can promote new

values, including the special status of their own positions.

The authority of a deity has also often been claimed by secular rulers to justify their judgements. Thus Hammurabi, a leader in Mesopotamia in the second millennium BCE, preceded his legal judgments (many of which we would see as far from just) by affirming that he had the authority of the gods (Bottéro, 1992). Such an example has resulted in conflict between secular and religious rulers as well as complicating the moral decisions of individuals. At the most basic level, in a modern religiously oriented society, would it be the duty of a member of a church to contribute to the maintenance of the church roof when his children need new shoes?

But there is a basic problem. Natural selection, favouring those who looked after their own interests, would favour individuals prone to selfish assertiveness. Why, then, should anyone ever be good? Why should individuals be nice to others with whom they are competing for scarce resources? It has seemed impossible to understand how natural selection could account for prosocial behaviour directed towards an unrelated potential competitor, but it is now apparent that several further mechanisms may have played a role.

*Parental care and nepotism*
The insights of Charles Darwin (1809-1882) and Alfred Russel Wallace (1823-1913) were that evolution occurs because individuals vary, leading to selection of those better able to survive and to rear more viable offspring than others and thereby pass on their genes to the next generation. In sexual reproduction, each of a couple's offspring will (on average) inherit half its genes from each parent. Parents who behaved prosocially to their offspring would be increasing the chances that their offspring survive to reproduce and that the next generation carries a higher proportion of their genes than those with parents who do not favour their own offspring (Price cited Harman, 2010; Haldane, 1932; Hamilton, 1964). Hence natural selection will favour parental care. However, there is a cost to parental care, in that parental care to one offspring will diminish the parent's capacity to look after others or later offspring. Generalising this to individuals less closely related than parents and offspring, an act may be advantageous to the actor in perpetuating genes identical with his own if the cost to him is less than half the benefit to his (the actor's full) sibling, a quarter the benefit to his grandchild, niece or nephew and, to an extent varying with the degree of relationship, to more distant relatives (Trivers, 1974). This

principle has now been confirmed in countless studies of animals and humans. A number of studies have shown that we do act preferentially towards our relatives: in China this has been formalised into a duty (Asma, 2013). For instance, in an experimental study requiring subjects to indicate which subjects they would save in a disaster, respondents in both the USA and Taiwan chose kin in preference to non-kin. They chose also friends rather than non-friends (Petrinovich, 1995), perhaps indicating that familiarity is a characteristic by which relatives are recognised. Giving preference to familiar others could, of course, be an effective base for the *genetic* selection of prosociality only in groups containing a fair proportion of blood relatives.

*Reciprocity*
A norm of reciprocity is not limited to revenge and goes a long way in explaining the dynamics of human personal relationships (review, Hinde, 1997). Under many circumstances, behaving prosocially to another human who behaves positively to you may pay off. Although prosocial reciprocity is rare in animals (Trivers 1985), in humans it has been recognised as a basis of morality in all cultures. Perhaps the human propensity to gossip helps us to identify individuals who are reliable reciprocators from amongst the other members of a group and select them as partners (indirect reciprocity). Variants of 'do-as-you-would-be-done-by' were emphasised by the founders of all the world's main religions and, in a meeting that led to 'Declaration of the Parliament of the World's Religions', variants of this 'Golden Rule' were universally accepted as basic to moral codes (Küng & Kuschel, 1993).

A group of individuals who always responded prosocially to others would be vulnerable to cheats so it is necessary, if the group is to persist, for cheats to be punished (Boyd & Richerson, 1992). 'Strong reciprocity' involves a willingness of group members to punish those who do not abide by group norms even though they do not profit from the act of punishing. The effects of a variety of variables on the maintenance of prosocial reciprocity in artificial games are discussed by Fehr & Fischbacher (2003). The Golden Rule tends to be related to the concept of 'fairness': what you do for others should equal what they do for you. This has given rise to a number of 'exchange theories'. None of the exchange theories is applicable everywhere without additional assumptions, but Equity Theory can be taken as an example. It has been formalised in several propositions (Walster et al. 1978):

i  Individuals tend to maximise what they can get. However, if everyone did this, society would be chaotic. Therefore
ii Groups work out systems for ensuring that rewards and costs are distributed equitably amongst individuals and usually do this by rewarding those who treat others equitably and punishing those who do not.
iii Individuals who find themselves to be inequitably treated become distressed and
iv Attempt to restore equity by manipulating their own perceived gains or costs or those of the other party.

This is a flexible scheme, but it can be used to account for many aspects of social behaviour. For instance an expression of gratitude can be seen as an appropriate and necessary response by an individual who gains as a consequence of another's costs. Of special interest in the current context are the facts that:
i  What an individual feels he deserves varies with his 'investments' in the sense of rank, beauty, wealth, etc.
ii It is possible, though much less common, for individuals to feel over-privileged as well as under-privileged in their relationships. For example, a sample of Dutch men and women were assessed for their perceptions of equity in their marriage, their marital satisfaction, and their desire to engage in extra-marital sex. Both women who felt themselves to be deprived and those who felt themselves to be over-benefited showed stronger desires for extra-marital sex than those who felt themselves to be in an equitable relationship. The difference was in the same direction but not significant for men (Prins, Buunk & van Yperen, 1993). This has been taken to imply that participants are guided by a 'social contract' requiring fairness (see also pp. 107-108). (There are, however, other explanations stemming from differing motivations between the partners).

In the real world, selfishness or nepotism often trumps fairness, and even when fairness is seen as crucial, the decision as to which criterion of fairness should be used is often elusive: for instance, a nepotistic desire to favour relatives may be directly contrary to a desire to be fair to all individuals.

A major issue arises, however, in equating the costs and benefits to the participants in a transaction. Fairness is a subjective issue, and in adult relationships the personalities of both partners matter: for instance, women pay themselves less than do men when allocating rewards between themselves and others, though it must be noted that generalisations from such experiments are likely to change over time with the world-view. The context may determine how far personal characteristics such as beauty, rank, celebrity status, etc. are seen as 'investments' (see above). What is considered fair also depends on what is exchanged: women rate aspects of relationships higher than do men (Foa & Foa, 1974). In allocating pieces of a cake that they have helped make, children's judgements change with age, passing through self-interest, equality (equal shares), equity (for instance, according to work put in) and social justice (need) (Lerner, 1981). In adult interactions we tend to be more generous to those whom we have seen to be generous to others – possibly because we hope they will behave generously to us in future interactions (Alexander, 1979, 1987; Nowak & Sigmund, 1998, 2005). (It should, of course, be emphasised that conclusions from experiments or observation in this area are liable to change with current conventions.)

*'Egalitarian' societies*
Evidence of another route by which prosociality may have been facilitated depends on studies of the evolution of social behaviour. Our closest relatives amongst non-human primates are the chimpanzees and gorilla. Chimpanzees that live south of the Congo river (pygmy chimpanzees) are unusual in that the males can be dominated by coalitions of females, but gorilla and common chimpanzees live in groups dominated by a single male or occasionally by a coalition of two males. It is probable that our humanoid ancestors, close relatives of these great apes, also lived in small groups led and dominated by a single individual (usually male). Males were larger than females, and any male or coalition of males who could establish dominance over the rest of the group could have priority of access to receptive females and other scarce resources. In the Great Apes (and presumably in our very early ancestors) an alpha male could take for himself a major share of the prey caught, leaving others to go hungry.

That this situation may not have been stable in early *Homo* species is suggested by evidence from studies of those societies of humans that have managed to survive in marginal habitats by a combination of hunting for meat (mostly by males) and gathering plant food (mostly by women). The habitats occupied by groups of hunter-gatherers stretch from the polar regions to equatorial tropical forests and deserts, and the details of their social arrangements vary. They live in quite small groups, and often resources are scarce. Individuals are in competition with each other for food, resting places, sexual partners, and so on. One might have expected, therefore, continuous conflict over these scarce resources, with individuals striving for the dominant position so that they could monopolise them. In fact anthropologists who have studied these societies have been impressed by their egalitarian nature. That does not mean that there is no conflict: rather any individual male with a tendency to show off or to be bossy is immediately taken down by others. Generalising broadly across diverse societies, in group discussions leading to decisions that will affect the group, no one individual is permitted to lead: the discussion is allowed to continue until some sort of consensus is reached. Everyone is conscious that pushiness will not be tolerated so that, for instance, a hunter who has been markedly successful is careful not to boast of his prowess, but plays down his success, saying that what he has killed was not a special specimen and not too difficult to trap or kill. An individual whose desire to put himself forward becomes obvious is put down by being ignored, ostracised, expulsion from the group or, in rare extreme cases, capital punishment.

Thus, while the selfish assertiveness of the individuals in a group is likely to lead to a tendency towards an hierarchical organisation, it may also lead to resentment amongst those who are not quite at the top, who can form coalitions leading to a more 'egalitarian system'. Data on the surviving populations of hunter-gatherers and some agriculturists confirm this picture. Hunter-gatherer bands are described as *'moral communities that agree on their values and, as a latent but potent political coalition, are always poised to manipulate or suppress political deviants'* (Boehm, 1991). In these marginal communities group action to put down an individual showing a tendency to bossiness is usually the result of considerable discussion. Gossiping plays a major role in their social dynamics (for further discussion, see p. 112).

Hold on, you will say, you cannot build a picture of human morality on the basis of evidence drawn from a few rather aberrant groups living in places where no one else wants to live. Social relationships differ between hunter/gather groups and over time, and the field data gathered by Boehm and a number of others have given rise to speculation about the precise psychological processes involved. Boehm's account explains the structure of hunter/gatherer groups in terms of conscious choices by those involved, while Erdal and Whiten (1994) ascribe fundamental importance to Machiavellian intelligence. I shall not pursue this issue: the only point I am making is that many of the psychological and behavioural propensities that made these egalitarian societies possible are present in us today (chapter 10), though the lack of emphasis we have put on them has all too obviously produced an entirely different, and from some perspectives a less desirable, result.

While equality, or at least the absence of conflict (see pp. 17-18), is a characteristic of many hunter-gatherer societies, this does not mean that there are no leaders: an individual with special skills may be allowed to lead temporarily over an issue in which his skill is of especial value, but his dominance will not spill over into other areas. Boehm (1991, 2012) ascribes the inability of any one to dominate to the 'love of personal freedom' of others who act pre-emptively to curb the social climbers. In his opinion the egalitarian ethos is internalised in all individuals as *'a set of strongly held moralistic positions about how life should be'* (Boehm, 2012, p. 68). In other words, the moral code is based on a shared desire that conflict should not become overt.

In relation to that, valuable resources are shared among the families in the group. A large animal is not consumed by the successful hunter's family but divided among the several families in the group (Kelly, 1995; Hill & Hurtado, 1996; Kaplan and Hill, 1985). This may have several beneficial consequences including reciprocity, inclusive fitness signalling that you are a sufficiently effective hunter to provide more than enough food for your household, long-term political conditions conducive to cooperative breeding, and shielding the families of the less good hunters in times of food scarcity and thereby maintaining the group's manpower (Wiessner, 2002).

*Inter-group conflict*
The issues mentioned so far may have been sufficient to reduce conflict within the group, but in doing so they may also have made the group more effective in competition with other groups. Each group must occasionally have had to compete with other groups for resources. Although biologists have long believed that competition between groups could have played no part in evolution (Williams, 1966), that view is now controversial in the case of human groups. It seems likely that selection takes place at many levels, including the individual: groups with a high proportion of individuals who were prosocial to and cooperated with their fellow group members, though not with members

of other groups, could out-compete those with fewer. This conclusion is based in part on artificial games, but supported by field observations: trapping small animals with nets could be more effective if a number of hunters cooperated by putting their nets out in a line in the forest, driving their prey into it and then sharing the meat, than if they placed the nets independently. In tackling large animals with spears or arrows, cooperation and sharing the meat must have been essential. In a review of his own field work and that of others on groups of surviving hunter-gatherers, Boehm (2012) has suggested that it was the necessity for cooperation in hunting that led to the replacement of groups dominated by a boss individual by a more egalitarian organisation.

Could a group consisting mainly of prosocial cooperating individuals not only be maintained but also win in competition with a group consisting mainly of selfish individuals? This view is still controversial. That such a mechanism seems not to operate in non-human animals renders it at first sight unlikely. Discussion of this issue has relied largely on mathematical models in which some individuals are seen as prosocial and others as selfishly assertive. In animals selection acts on genetic differences between individuals; but in humans differences between individuals are passed on largely by non-genetic, cultural means. Could such differences between groups remain stable? Would not the differences disappear through cross-group marriage, copying or other forms of cultural diffusion? Boyd & Richerson (1992; 2005) have shown that a modelling approach indicates that cultural selection could be effective if naïve individuals tended to copy the behaviour that was most common in the group, if the environment were heterogeneous, and if the groups tended to move about from time to time. These conditions are likely to be satisfied in groups of hunter-gatherers (e.g. Boyd & Richerson, 2002). Thus, cultural group selection is at least possible and does not necessarily imply warfare between the groups, but competition for scarce resources.

There is, however, a problem. It would be necessary for the norm of cooperation to be maintained by the punishment of those who did not conform. A group whose members were all prosocial to each other would be vulnerable to free-riders, that is, to individuals who pretended to conform to the group norm of prosociality with other group members yet not bearing the costs of doing so. Boyd & Richerson (1992, 2005) have shown that for groups of predominantly prosocial individuals to be maintained, any individual who did not conform must be punished.

This means that individuals in predominantly prosocial groups would not be favoured by selection if they all ceased to punish other group members who did not follow group norms: what matters to each individual is that *others* should behave prosocially, not that he or she should. It could thus be to his or her advantage to punish group members who did not behave prosocially, provided that the costs of punishing were less than the gains. (He himself would be open to punishment by others if he did not behave prosocially to them). Computer modelling shows that, in sizeable groups, strategies involving cooperation, punishing non-cooperators, and punishing those who do not punish non-cooperators can be stable if the costs of being punished are large enough (Boyd & Richerson, 2005; Santos et al. 2011). Though anecdotal evidence indicates that the perception of fair dealing is rewarding (Clayton & Lerner, 1991), punishing involves costs to the punisher and the nature of the selection that ensures that the punisher could accept the costs of punishing is controversial (Bowles et al 2010; Henrich & Boyd, 2001). Most probably the punisher is compensated because he acquires a good reputation and is therefore more likely to be helped in future interactions or to succeed in competition for mates.

One must, of course, remember that there are many differences between mathematical models and real life. Most obviously, individuals are not either prosocial co-operators or selfishly assertive, but are capable of adjusting their behaviour according to circumstances. An individual who is gentle and caring to members of his own group in times of plenty may change if resources become scarce. In many human societies dependent on agriculture, dominance relations may be far from simple, with males apparently dominant in the political forum but females in the kitchen (Hinde, 2002). Nevertheless, the predictions of these mathematical models are borne out by the surviving hunter-gatherers, and we shall see (Chapter 10) that the behavioural propensities on which they depend are present in ourselves.

These models suggest that in early human groups, behaviour to other members of the same group would inevitably have involved ambivalence. There would have been competition over resources that were scarce, leading individuals to behave with selfish assertiveness towards other members of their group. However, there would also have been a propensity to cooperate with other in-group members and behave positively to them if this led to greater success for the group in competition with rival groups. Punishment of in-group members who did not conform would be necessary. This implies a need for balance in behaviour to members of your own group. A group in which the members were over-prosocial would be open to penetration by free-riders: there must therefore have been some limit to the extent of prosociality. The righteous indignation of the co-operators at non-cooperative behaviour would lead to the punishment of the non-cooperators. At the same time, a group whose members were wholly selfishly assertive would soon disintegrate. Hence the view that morality plays a large part in holding a balance between these two propensities in relations with in-group members (Figure 2).

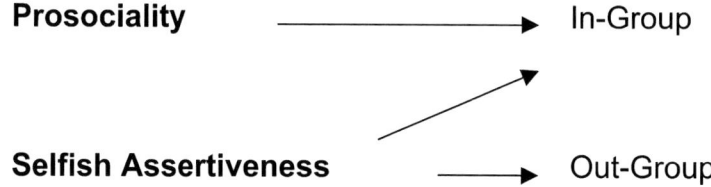

**Figure 2.** Differential influences of natural and cultural selection on the direction of prosocial and selfish propensities towards the 'in-group' vs. an 'out-group'.

Thus morality is to be equated not just with being good, but with being appropriately good. This is in harmony with the view of our conscience (pp. 49-50) not just as something that stops us being bad but as something that tells how far we can go in either direction without incurring too much moral indignation in others (Alexander, 1979, 1987). There is support for this in our contempt for goody-goodies. Indeed the value placed on assertiveness/non-assertiveness has varied not only between cultures but also over time within cultures. For example, in English-speaking countries feminists have tried to encourage women to develop their assertiveness so that they can compete on equal terms with men.

This model suggests that there would be no selection for prosociality towards an out-group. This is in harmony with experience, but raises the question of how the in-group is defined. There can be no simple criterion by which group differences are perceived: a little thought shows that characteristics that have been used to mark distinctions over which people have been willing to kill each other are trivial compared with what they have in common as human beings. Practically any difference may be manipulated by warmongers and reified by icons and rhetoric. The most hopeful course for those who would prevent physical conflict is to minimise differences and emphasise humanity, though it is seldom as easy as that.

**Summary**
The dichotomy between 'instinct' and 'learning' no longer provides a satisfactory framework for the origin of psychological propensities.

Prosociality and selfish assertiveness arose through the action of selection, natural or cultural.

Some factors likely to be important in the evolution of prosociality are summarised.

Morality holds the balance between prosocial and selfishly assertive propensities.

The nature of that balance is likely to differ between societies.

Chapter 4

# Why Behave Morally?

Many people assume that our morality depends on religion. This is epitomised by the story of Moses coming down from the mountain with the Ten Commandments inscribed on tablets of stone. Since the Commandments contain an admonition to respect the religious specialists and to behave prosocially, it is a reasonable presumption that it was in the interests of the prophets and priests, whose existence and status depended on the maintenance of the current sacred system, to support their divine origin. However, times change, and there are at least two reasons for regarding religious belief and morality as independent issues:

## Independent origins of belief and morality*

Religious belief has had and has certain beneficial consequences, particularly in providing a way to explain otherwise inexplicable events, in giving comfort to individuals in stressful situations, and perhaps most importantly in providing a meaning in life. These consequences of belief have so far been the province of novelists, poets, playwrights and the visual arts. They are important because they call attention to the existence of human potentials for prosociality of many kinds (Dormor, 2008), but seem not to provide clear guidelines for understanding their nature. Morality, by contrast, is significant primarily in ensuring the harmonious nature of interpersonal relationships and groups that are so important at every stage in human evolution (Dennett, 1997; Hinde, 1997, 1999, 2002) and it is vital that we get to understand its nature. There is also now considerable overlap in the beneficial consequences of religious belief and morality: morality may be manipulated to affirm the rectitude of religious belief and morality may be used to enhance the comfort provided by religion. But the view that they were selected primarily for different beneficial consequences suggests that there is less reason for regarding either as providing a firm basis for the other.

## Does religious belief have beneficial consequences for morality?

Does being religious imply that an individual will behave more morally than one who is not? Clearly this is a tricky area of research: what does 'being religious' imply and can it be measured? Furthermore, most of

---
\* *See recent analysis by McKay & Whitehouse, in press, Psychological Bulletin, 2015.*

the studies involve self-reports: that people who *say they are religious* also *say* that they live moral lives is no big surprise. Many studies are correlational: no such study can show that religion causes prosociality, that prosociality fosters religion, neither or both. Some studies do report a positive relation between religiosity and prosociality in experimental situations. However a meta-analysis, putting all known reputable studies together, provides a fairly clear picture. There is strong evidence that individuals *who describe themselves* as religious, for instance claiming to pray and go to church, also *describe themselves* as prosocial. But that is a different matter from behaving prosocially. Most studies of the relations between *external assessments* of moral behaviour (rather than individuals' perceptions of their own behaviour) and religiosity show that individuals describing themselves as religious do not behave significantly more prosocially than those who do not so describe themselves (Norenzayan & Sharif, 2008). For instance, in an experimental approach, subjects in a hurry were caused to pass by a confederate lying on the sidewalk and obviously needing help. There was no evidence that those who claimed to be religious were more likely to help than those who did not claim religiosity (Darley & Batson, 1973). However, helping in this study was recorded unobtrusively. There is evidence to show that individuals are more likely to behave prosocially if they know they are being observed or if the individual's reputation in his own eyes or those of others could be enhanced by prosocial behaviour. Some experimental evidence has shown that children and adults are more apt to behave honestly if they think they are being watched (Bateson et al., 2006; Nettle et al., 2012; Sharif & Norenzayan, 2007; McKay et al., 2011). This, of course, is compatible with the preceding discussion of exchange theory and could be related to indirect reciprocity. It could have nothing to do with religious belief: people behave prosocially if doing so makes them seem suitable persons to deal with.

Thus, it must not be assumed that an apparent effect of religion on prosociality is due to religious belief: it may be due to the social component of religiosity (Shor & Roelf, 2013). The evidence is that the assumed association between religious belief and prosocial behaviour could make those who feel religious both believe that they are good and be good if they believe themselves to be observed by others, and perhaps especially if they believe themselves to be observed by a deity. But to what extent religious belief leads of itself to more moral behaviour is not yet clear (e.g. Johnson, 2005; see also Hackney &

Sanders, 2003; Hannay, 1980). The atheist and agnostic have to face the question of whether religious belief, though false, should be encouraged because it makes people feel that they are being watched and therefore behave better (cf. Dawkins, 2006).

## The conscience

Given acceptance of moral rules, how do individuals choose between doing good or bad? Hume (e.g. 1739/1969) considered that we have a moral sense with an evaluative mechanism. We refer to the latter as the conscience, whose nature can be understood as follows. In interpreting people's behaviour, including our own, we use a concept of 'self'. Our behaviour and how we see ourselves changes with time and situation, but we explain the continuity by postulating that we each have a 'self'. Humans take a few years to acquire a sense of self and it seems to be primarily, but not exclusively, a human characteristic. Although we see the 'self' as explaining continuity, how we describe ourselves varies with time and situation. Thus, a woman psychologist in the company of female non-psychologists will describe herself primarily as a psychologist, but in the company of male psychologists is more prone to describe herself as a woman (McGuire & McGuire, 1988).

As part of the self we also hold certain values or rules by which we evaluate behaviour. 'Having a bad conscience' can be seen as corresponding to a discrepancy between the values internalised in the self-system and the actions one sees oneself as having taken or as about to take. Experimental data indicates that we are sensitive to discrepancies between the values in our self-concept and how we see ourselves to be behaving or intending to behave or how we perceive others to perceive us (Backman, 1988). If one sees oneself behaving or about to behave in a manner that is incompatible with our values we feel guilt or shame, and may change our behaviour (Lewis, 1992). If an individual perceives a lack of congruency in his behaviour, he may use a variety of devices to restore it. For instance, he may change his behaviour, or his memory of the event may become distorted, or he may blame others and so on (Backman, 1988). What matters for congruency, it must be noted, is how those involved perceive the situation, not what they actually do. Thus congruency can be restored by believing 'it was his fault really' or adopting similar excuses.

What we are concerned with, therefore, are the values that each individual has stored in his mind/brain. As we have seen, these are acquired largely through experience in the culture in which the individual lives, and thus may differ between cultures. In so far as our decisions for action involve achieving a balance between prosociality and selfish assertiveness, that is between our own interests and those of the society in which we live, I suggest our current values are inclined too much towards self-interest. The European/ North American view of self is of a limited entity, one entity amongst many interrelated but separate individuals. This is very different from the views of self held for example in many other societies, especially in East Asian societies. In 'individualistic' societies, such as those in Europe and North America, people tend to see the self as developing in a nexus of other selves, but maturing into an entity that sees itself as distinct from other selves. In collectivist societies people tend to see themselves as strongly identified with, and with obligations to and from, the family and other groups such as the company for which they work or their blood relatives (see p. 115). This is the result of the way they were reared – to be sensitive to their mother's feelings with an expectation that their mothers will be sensitive to their own needs and feelings. This sense of mutual dependency has been called 'amae'. The child depends on the mother to satisfy its needs, and the satisfaction of the child's needs satisfies the mother's. This can be extended outside the family with mutual identification between individual and group. For instance, self-esteem may be more closely related to the success of the group than with individual success (review, Lewis, 1992).

## Intuition or rational debate?

This model of the conscience makes it sound as though there is a rational debate inside our minds in which we make rational comparisons between, for instance, how we explain to ourselves what we are doing and what we intuitively feel we should be doing. This reflects the long-standing debate among both philosophers and psychologists as to whether we come to moral decisions intuitively or by the use of rational argument. I do not propose to review that argument here: experimental evidence suggests that intuition usually comes first and may then be immediately provided with a rational justification. That does not mean that, in situations calling for moral judgement, intuitions determine what we do, but they usually come first and the reasoning we use to justify our intuition-based actions may be self-justificatory (e.g. Haidt, 2012).

We are born with a capacity to learn to make moral judgements. Some moral rules (principles) are little influenced by experience, while others (precepts, conventions) are strongly affected by the actor's cultural background, current situation, experience and so on. To take one example, virtually all moral systems forbid the killing of a member of one's own group, but permit and even praise killing of members of enemy groups in war. Infanticide is permitted in some groups where the mother is unlikely to be able to rear her baby (Scheper-Hughes, 1992), and some groups that believe that you enter the next world in the same state in which you leave this one see it as proper to put elderly parents to death (Benedict, 1934).

Intuitions and rational calculations do not always coincide. Experiments, either in a laboratory or using subjects from the general public and conducted over the internet, have involved scenarios in which the subject had to choose whether or not to act to save several lives when doing so would sacrifice the life of another individual: on the basis of such experiments Hauser (2006) concluded that subjects see it as not permissible to cause another harm even if that harm is used as a means to a greater good, but it is permissible if the harm is only a foreseen consequence of intending to cause a greater good. In practice this is a distinction not easy to make.

The experimental evidence from these 'trolley-type' experiments (see Hauser, 2006) suggests that what matters in our distinction between good and bad actions are the intentions behind the actions. But, while attention to intentions provides important criteria by which to assign praise or blame, it is not as straightforward as that. Most moral decisions are far from simple and involve not a dichotomous decision but selection between a number of considerations.

An evolutionary approach to the nature of morality implies (probably cultural) selection for discriminating between behaviour that is and is not acceptable. Since societies differ one must expect moral issues to differ between societies, and the criteria of moral behaviour not to be rigid. We are all involved in the dynamics of changes in morality because we are constantly choosing between alternative ways of behaving. The Golden Rule is ubiquitous possibly because it has been selected continuously over the years: the rule against premarital cohabitation is in danger of disappearing because it is not observed.

None of this, I realise, concerns what goes through one's mind when trying to justify action. When I asked someone why she made prosocial decisions when confronted with moral problems, she produced the following list:
a)      The individual's self-image: 'I am an honourable person and

therefore I must do the honourable thing'.
b) Role models, such as thinking what would my mother (or Jesus) have done.
c) Positive social identification, such as the idea that people from Cambridge/England/the UK do or do not do that sort of thing.
d) Past experience of community action with positive consequences.
e) Hope of reward in this life or an imagined other.
f) Fear of retribution.
(L. Adams, personal communication)

**Summary**
Religious stories are unlikely to be true. But religious belief and practice are profoundly important for many people. Religious beliefs probably arose through our propensity to ascribe events to agents, especially human-like agents. Prosocial propensities probably had a number of sources, including parental care, nepotism and reciprocity, and the greater success of groups with prosocial members in inter-group conflict, as seen in hunter-gatherer groups.

Since religious belief and morality have separate origins, there is no special reason for thinking that belief can supply a sound basis for morality. The evidence that religiosity is related to more prosocial behaviour is equivocal.

The nature of the conscience is considered briefly.

# Part III
# Change is Necessary

The following chapters concern some background issues that must be taken into account as we formulate our goals (chapter 5), the nature of the morality we seek (chapter 6), some issues that are partly responsible for our present state (chapters 7-9), and finally evidence that change is possible (chapters 10-11).

Chapter 5

# Background for Change

**The task is not easy**
It is easy to paint a picture of a Utopian future, where the sources of our problems have been recognised and dealt with, and we all live in harmony with our fellow humans. But it cannot be like that. The sources of our malaise are deep-seated and require changes in how we see the world. Many will say that it is either arrogant or hopeless to try to change societal values, but the answer lies in the current state of our societies: we just *must* change our ways.

We have the capacity to build a better world (Chapter 10), but it will take time. We shall need to be patient, content with nudging things in the right direction, and setting our sights on reaching our goals in a lifetime or so.

At the societal level our problems are not helped by the tendency of democratically elected politicians to focus on what they perceive the electorate to want for the next election. That is one reason why individuals, the 'man/woman in the street', are so important. In the long run, the responsibility is on us, every one of us. Whatever happens, we must not despair.

Values really can change: there have been dramatic changes (admittedly mainly for the worse) in values in my lifetime. There was a time (and this is not just harking back to the Good Old Days) when you could be pretty hopeful that if you dropped your wallet, someone would hand it in to the police station; or if a shopkeeper gave too much change, the customer would return it. In Cambridge the Sunday papers were left in a pile on the pavement with a cap beside them: it was assumed that if you took a paper you would put the money in the cap. Not so today. I do not want to make a generalisation here about changes in morality over time: in some ways society may be more moral and in some ways less moral, and much depends on the criteria you use, the time span over which the comparison is made, and on where you live. I might think differently if I had lived in, say, District 6 in Cape Town or the Gorbals of Glasgow in the 1940s, or in parts of Mumbai today. And, as I mentioned in chapter 1, there are signs that in some respects things are improving: slavery and capital punishment are being abolished, and the evils of poverty are recognised. If we really want a better world we must use a medium-length time frame.

## Goals must be limited

One must accept that a perfect and universally acceptable moral code is beyond our reach. By the nature of things, prosociality and selfish assertiveness towards other members of one's community will always be in conflict (pp. 44-45). Cultures are so different, people are so different, times change, new problems are constantly arising. A morality promoting social well-being in one society might not fit another living in a different environment and with a different history. Many of the problems that societies face are new problems, arising from scientific advances and cultural changes. Old rules cannot always be trusted. In the modern world, leaving many descendants, giving preference to one's kin, or pushing the interests of one's kin group, are no longer seen as proper or as natural as they used to be. In any case individuals and institutions are adept at finding let-outs to almost any moral rule. So we must accept that there can be no absolute moral code, valid for all people at all places in all times. However, moral values must be derived from shared views about how other members of our society should behave in the interests of social harmony, so a morality must be based in human propensities that are conducive to that end, with the flexibility to cope with the inevitable changes in society.

Current codes are likely to have been based on aspirations that served well in the past, and may serve as a starting point for the future. But the present is not like the past, and the precise shape of the future is not predictable. Our morality must adjust. Institutions respected by many, like the Christian Church, are unlikely to embrace change readily. And, of course, the advocate for change must always ask whether he/she is biased in his certainty that he is right and the rest of society is wrong. No moral system, or indeed secular law, will necessarily be the best or fairest for all the people in a society: it may be engineered by one sub-group in order to bind others to its will, or it may be a botched-up code compromising what is believed to be best for several different sub-groups. Some tension is inevitable, and change is sometimes proper (Hinde, 2004b).

## Materialism

At present the curbs on selfish assertiveness are weak: prosociality and care for the community take a back seat. Asserting your own needs or wishes is seen as the way to get on: greed is everywhere, and is both a cause and a result of the excessive materialism that surrounds us. The psychological bases are only partially understood, but the accumulation of possessions may be related to insecurity (Jarrett, 2013). Those who have want more, and much of our society is directed to creating new things for us to want. In our materialist society, advertisers blur the gap between needing and wanting. There seems to be no limit to the things some people feel they must have. In part because the more you have, the easier it is to get more, the gap between rich and poor increases (see pp. 78-80).

How can people be made to see that for much of what that they get, the probability is that someone else gets less? How can recognition of the difference between 'want' and 'need' become second nature? The necessary changes in our outlook will not be achieved easily, but they will never happen if we do not start to work for them now.

## Conflict is inevitable

Some conflict between individual autonomy and the social order is inevitable. As we have seen, morality holds a balance between prosociality and selfish assertiveness. Individuals tend to assert their own interests, but inevitably these are sometimes contrary to group interests. In any case, there will always be cheats, and if the balance favoured prosociality too far, there would be no way to thwart the cheats, and society could be taken over by free-riders. The law can be seen in part as an attempt to underwrite rationally the precepts, prohibitions and values of a moral code, ensuring a balance between prosociality and selfish assertiveness by punishing excesses of the latter (Hinde, 2002; 2004b).

Nearly every morally significant decision we make involves conflict between incompatible considerations. It may be just an internal matter: do I have time to stop and help the needy traveller lying by the road? It may be pragmatic: does a child with an incurable disease have as much right to a limited resource as a healthy child with the prospect of a constructive life ahead of her? Perhaps values conflict: it is wrong to kill, but could I help to stop a greater evil by joining the army? Individuals' duties may conflict with societal morality: perhaps one feels that one has a duty to one's employer that conflicts with spending time with one's family. A list of possible conflicts would be almost endless (Hinde, 2002). Simple rules will not provide adequate guidance, life is unavoidably full of contradictions, and there is seldom a simple choice between right and wrong. The question must be not 'Am I breaking a rule?' but 'Does what I propose to do contribute to or detract from general well-being?' recognising that the answer is often context dependent and often not susceptible to a yes or no answer. Rules have their value but must be seen as one way of characterising morality, not as its essence.

Thus, morality must be *seen as* absolute, but the very complexity of most moral decisions means that it must have some flexibility. In any group we must cooperate with each other but, if any resource is scarce, we are likely to compete with each other. Conflict is inevitable, and must not be swept under the carpet. It is too easy to believe the tension to be reduced by perceiving the matter to have been settled or one's own behaviour to be correct. Over minor issues in personal relationships tension can be minimised by the mechanisms that maintain congruence in the self-system (p. 49): one can reinterpret or misperceive or re-evaluate one's own behaviour or the opinions of one's critics so that any lack of congruency is removed (Backman, 1988). But such solutions may not be durable.

**Blinkered views**
With cultural norms as they are, none of us is immune to their influence, and that includes you and me. It is too easy to be blind to the suffering of those whom the present system drives into poverty. And, as I wrote in Chapter 1, it is difficult for those who live in a first world country to even imagine the lot of many in sub-Saharan Africa. Just try to think what it must be like to live in a community where infanticide is accepted because half-starved mothers are unlikely to be able to rear a child, or where food and clean water are difficult to obtain and there can be no hope that things will ever be better. But it need not be so.

More egalitarian societies will be possible when a more egalitarian society is the accepted goal (see pp. 108-112). Change is possible, but will not be achieved overnight (Holloway, 1999). We do not yet know enough to deal with all the problems, but we must not let idealism sink in the sea of reality.

**Is morality passé?**
Many may say that it is no good fiddling with morality, that is old-fashioned stuff and nobody bothers with it now. That of course is the point; it is just because people disregard morality that we are in this situation. Such people may go on to say that the problems lie in our political and economic systems: if we had a different political, economic or financial system people would behave more responsibly, or there would be less crime, or fewer teenage pregnancies. But, as I

argued in Part 1, causation is not solely one way. It is central to the thesis of this book that how individuals behave, what they value, their culture and political and economic systems, are interconnected, each affecting the others. This was illustrated in Figure 1: how people behave is affected by the political and business/commercial systems, and also affects the nature of those systems.

There is always plenty of discussion about our political and economic systems, but too little about our values and morality. The values we respect should be crucial in shaping our financial and political systems. We must attempt to redress the balance, starting from the bottom level of how people behave and the values they hold. If they are changed in a manner that is conducive to the 'general good', political and economic systems that also are conducive to the same ends will be easier to find.

However, such is human greed and ingenuity, loopholes will be found in every system. To get to the heart of the matter, it is not enough to draft systems that cope with human greed. Rather, we must also encourage the positive side of human nature. That means a change in world-view to one in which the 'common good' is seen as a goal at least comparable to 'own good'. Many will say that you cannot change human nature, or that such a goal is ephemeral. I suggest that there is a more positive side of human nature waiting to be released.

**Is the time ripe?**

In spite of religion's many problems, the time may not be ripe simply to discourage religion: its stories may not be true but they provide comfort to many and there may be no need to take that away precipitously. Beliefs too firmly held can do much harm, but the stories contain lessons of importance for modern society. The anti-theists want the abolition of religion: I wonder if society is ready for such a change?

One can say something similar about morality. We must learn from the floundering attempts to impose western type democracy on Iraq and Afghanistan: democracy can flourish only if certain types of societal structures, behaviour and values are there already. You cannot impose a particular brand of morality on any society any time anywhere (Hinde & Rotblat, 2003). But that is not what I am proposing. What we need is first an understanding of the nature of morality. As we understand more, we shall see what adjustments are needed in our culture and how they are to be made. Some suggestions are made in the remaining chapters.

**Summary**
If we want to build a world with less tension, we must be optimistic and start with limited goals, nudging our current system away from the excessive materialism that we have today. We must not be too optimistic: change for the better will take a generation or two. Conflict is inevitable, and rigid rules are less likely to be useful than values and goals. We must focus on values rather than precepts about what to do and what not to do.

# Chapter 6
# Towards a New Morality

## How we see the world

The aim must be not to abandon the system of morality that we have at present, but to see how it can be adjusted for the modern world. The key, I suggest, lies in asking how do we, and those around us, see the world?

We often see our outlook on the world as influenced by our leaders. When things are going wrong, we seek to change leaders or the political party in charge, or we may attempt to adjust the financial system or some other internal institution. But we must also remember that others are influenced by how we behave. Everything that we do may affect the world-views of others. If we are seen to bully our colleagues, others may be more likely to see the world as made up of bullies and may try to emulate them. If you are seen to be honest, others may be encouraged to be honest too. Of course, it may go the other way, but the point is that how every one of us behaves makes a contribution to the way in which others see the world. Thus, how you behave matters. This means taking a 'bottom-up' approach, as illustrated in Fig. 1.

World-views are influenced by experience from early in life. Young children have propensities to be good as well as bad, to please their parents as well as to behave with selfish assertiveness (Eisenberg & Fabes, 1998)(See above). Which predominates is largely a result of the child's experiences not only in its family of origin (pp. 32-33), but also in the wider society into which it is born: the evils we now see in society are at least partly the consequence of the social environments we have created and are experienced by our children. And the complications are endless.

The nature of our society must therefore carry at least some of the responsibility for the behaviour of individuals. Poverty and wealth differences are not only conducive to crime (pp. 78-80), but also create family situations that make it difficult for parents to show the combination of loving care and sensitive discipline that will produce children who will become adults who will rear their children with greater sensitivity to what children need if they are to become responsible citizens and parents in their turn (pp. 95-97). But the reverse is also true: the behaviour and values of individuals are responsible for the nature of society. To break this vicious circle we need a change in the way in which individuals see the world, and for that it is necessary to work at both ends of the dialectic, from the bottom up as well as from the top down (Fig. 1). We need changes in both the influences of opinion-makers on individuals and of individuals on those who influence society.

**Carrot and stick**
Differences in beliefs lead to conflict between religious systems, so our future morality should be independent of particular sets of religious beliefs. Where then, you may ask, will the carrot and stick formerly provided by Heaven and Hell come from? The answer is that incentives and brakes are already part of social living. We already have propensities to punish other individuals if we disapprove of their behaviour and to reward those who behave well. Gossip spreads the news about good or bad behaviour. Righteous indignation by our peers can take the place of our real or unconscious fear of divine punishment for wrong-doing: in every society those who defy the accepted norms are likely to be ostracised, punished or rejected. Equally, approval by our fellows can act as an incentive. Those whose behaviour is exemplary according to societal norms are respected, receive adulation, or have statues erected in their honour. Heaven and hell are redundant.

In hunter-gatherers absence of overt conflict is maintained by such social forces, but the size and complexity of modern societies reduces their effectiveness. At present, the expression of righteous indignation is frequently suppressed for fear of being seen as self-righteous or hypocritical, and seeking for the approval of one's peers can be seen as a sign of weakness. It is necessary to take a more balanced view, restoring a degree of righteous indignation at the aberrant behaviour of one's fellows, sensitivity to their disapproval, and pride in their approval of more appropriate values and behaviour. Of course, one may be wrong in how one interprets a situation and one must recognise that one may be wrong, but humility must not be over-valued.

At present it is too easy to let things go, to shrug one's shoulders and say 'He is doing the best he can'. We must not be too afraid of stating our values. Are we thinking that an increased impact of the disapproval by one's fellows might imply an on-going state of tension in society? Over time, as the prevailing world-outlook changes and more communal norms become embedded in peoples' self-systems, we could hope for a reduction in this tension.

## An absolute or a flexible morality?

The image of the Ten Commandments carved in stone and brought down from Mount Sinai by Moses implies that our moral rules are immutable: this would have been attractive to moral leaders in part because sin would then be easily identifiable. Every day most people tend to think of morality in terms of 'Do nots' or 'Do's': 'Do not kill', 'Do not tell lies', 'Do be kind to the old and to small children'. That is fine, but we are beginning to find that we need a morality focusing on values. The complexity of modern life and our own nature means that many decisions that we make involve conflict between incompatible moral demands, and judgements in terms of simple rules or even intentions are often inadequate.

The perception that we must try to live by the rules that have held our society together for millennia makes intuitive sense: clearly rules must be *perceived as* immutable, otherwise it would be easy to find reasons for not attending to them. A moral code must be universally acceptable and moral values must be seen as absolute. But in apparent contradiction to this, a moral code must have some limited flexibility, for the moral problems with which individuals are faced are seldom simple, and may demand accommodation. The complexity of our societies results in a host of problems in which moral rules that are generally recognised in the society seem to conflict. For instance, who has not felt that to 'bear false witness' might be the moral thing to do because it would avoid someone's unhappiness? Again, one may feel that one should help another who is sick or disabled, but to do so might affront the other's self-esteem. Or it is immoral to steal, but would it be immoral to steal a drug that was otherwise unobtainable if it would save one's wife's life?

When, if ever, is a lie justified? Is it better to be bluntly factual in telling a father that his son has had an accident, giving one's news an edge of optimism? Or that he died instantly and did not suffer, although that was not the case? The answer must surely depend on circumstances and the personalities of those involved: simple rules are unlikely to be adequate.

At the risk of being repetitive, here is another example of dialectical changes in moral value. At one time it was quite respectable to own slaves. Indeed, owning slaves was rationalised in many ways – for instance many claimed that by exposing them to Christian teaching, slaves, seen as inferior beings, were lifted out of their state of ignorance and offered salvation. In the UK the change came from the efforts of a few individuals, notably Wilberforce and Clarkson, who were successful in swinging UK workers' opinions against the slave trade (see p. 117).

Yet another example is the current focus on paedophilia. A few years ago it was discovered that a well respected entertainer, already dead, had been sexually exploiting the children with whom his work brought him into contact. It soon appeared that many others were aware of what was going on, but had said nothing, largely because the entertainer's prestige seemed to make him immune to criticism and his activities were accepted as, although reprehensible, 'what some people did' and was best not talked about. But, once public, more and more victims gained the courage to come forward to testify against him, other offenders were exposed, and the whole climate of opinion changed.

Our need for a morality based on values has been especially evident in the field of reproductive biology. Is abortion, involving the killing of a potential human being, justified because it saves the mother's life or enables her to realise her potential in other ways? Feelings have been so strong that, in the USA, a doctor practising in an abortion clinic was murdered. Is this an issue about which a woman should be allowed to make up her own mind? 'No' comes the answer, the foetus is not able to articulate its claim to life. Well then, does its claim matter? Does it know it has a claim? And so the argument goes on, but the bottom line is that the anti-abortionists claimed the authority of a Holy Book whose authority on this issue was not recognised by their opponents. However, for legal and other reasons it was necessary to specify an age at which a foetus achieved personhood, and for largely anatomical and physiological reasons that was agreed to be 14 days (Warnock, 2004).

Again, is artificial insemination with a donor's sperm permissible? What are the consequences for the offspring? Such questions are difficult to answer, and many fall back on their interpretations of the Bible or other Holy Book whose validity is not recognised by their opponents.

Today we can see the beliefs and ethical aspects of a religious system coming apart as modern Catholics try to keep their key beliefs and respect for the Church in spite of its views on the ordination of women and contraception and its lack of oversight on priests taking advantage of those in their charge. Churches cannot allow their moralities to diverge too far from the changes in practice in secular society, or the churches fall into disrepute. However, from a recent Papal statement on the use of condoms it seems as though the Roman Catholic Church is having to soften its teaching in response to what the public believes and does. Since the election of the current Roman Catholic Pope, it is becoming clear that the new power at the top of this hierarchical organisation wishes to change its image.

On a longer time-scale, flexibility is necessary also to strike a proper balance between controlling and accommodating to changes in society. As I have stressed, times change and values change. Moral aims must be to some degree congruent with the society, and society with the moral values. The necessity for flexibility should not surprise Jews, Christians or Muslims, for the Old Testament is after all a history of change. And St. Paul's letters pointed out the need for change in the way in which people then lived.

Nevertheless some rules are nearly ubiquitous, perhaps because they are rooted in existing codes, which are rooted in turn in our nature. Reciprocal exchange, and some variant of the Golden Rule of 'do-as-you-would-be-done-by', are probably basic to all cultures. We value 'fairness' in all exchanges. Ultimately, we deplore environmental pollution in part because it may affect us or our descendants: the polluters are receiving benefits that far outstrip their own costs, while imposing costs on others. Again, it is possible for a financier to become unbelievably rich while convincing himself that he has not broken any of the moral rules of our society. This is partly the result of the role of institutions in our society, discussed in chapters 7 and 8. But it also requires focusing on the consequences for others of what one does as well as its consequences for oneself. In the end, if some get richer, it is highly likely that others will get poorer. We are unhappy about the excessive incomes of some people in the commercial and financial sections not only because we are envious but because of the effects of wealth differentials on so many aspects of society (pp. 78-80). I am suggesting, as many have done before, that the way forward is a greater emphasis on the well-being of the community and less on self-advancement.

A moral code is pointless unless it restricts personal freedom, yet personal freedom is widely valued. A balance must be found: a code based solely on permitting total personal freedom would lead inevitably to social disharmony and perhaps to overpopulation; but too much emphasis on social uniformity could lead to the demise of individuality. A delicate balance is necessary: moral codes can vary only between limits if societies are to be viable.

## Criteria

The distinction between 'good' and 'bad' behaviour is often difficult for both the religious and the non-religious. We can no longer automatically accept all Biblical dictates – they may have fitted an iron-age culture, but not always today's. In any case, it is seldom a case of black or white, and behaviour that would be condemned in normal circumstances may be condoned in others. So are there no hard criteria by which to distinguish between good and bad? Killing is almost universally proscribed, and yet in some cultures killing can be partially condoned if it can be described as a *crime passionel*, and in some areas of extreme poverty infanticide by neglect is accepted because the mother is seen as unable to rear the baby (Scheper-Hughes, 1992). If a woman gave birth in the Auschwitz Nazi concentration camp, the guards killed both mother and baby: the prisoners therefore decided to kill newborn babies to save the mother's life (Des Pres, 1976). In English law the degree of guilt is recognised and indicated by the severity of the sentence, which can be reduced by extenuating circumstances.

As we have seen, a general guide is whether the intent behind the action involves the good of the group or only that of the individual actor. But if a rich person donates a large sum to charity hoping that it will bring public acclaim, is that 'good' behaviour? Is his behaviour more virtuous than that of the poor man who gives only a few pence? Here is another problem: in the short term it is what people *do* that determines the nature of society, but in the longer term their motivations or intentions may be more important by virtue of the example they give to others. This is implied in the Tenth Commandment, where it is *coveting* that is proscribed (Exodus, 20:17). In the real world the distinction between good and bad is seldom clear-cut, and it is usually a case of more or less.

That is all very well, but in the real world we do make judgements, so can we not make any generalisations about the nature of goodness? According to the model I have been using, our intuitions come from criteria already stored, acquired from observation of the behaviour of others and the teaching of parents and mentors. In the longer term the criteria acquired in this way come from a dialectic between the judgements made by members of one's reference group in the past and how people actually behave (see pp. 24-27).

As we have seen, in so far as our judgements of the behaviour of actors in the past have a criterion in common, they result from selection acting to promote a balance between the well-being of the community or group and its members, and the well-being of the actor. Thus, in general behaviour that profits oneself but harms others is proscribed, while that which benefits others in one's group (especially if it does not benefit the self) is to be encouraged.

This (admittedly over-simple) generalisation implies that what is seen as good depends on the reference group. Suicide is wrong, but self-immolation as a protest against a corrupt (in your eyes) regime may be seen by peers as an example of supreme goodness. Murdering a camp guard, a representative of self-interested oppressors, may be seen by fellow prisoners as just. Such cases imply that the search for absolutes is a delusion. This view, that moral judgements on specific issues are culture- and situation-dependent, may not be what we would like to feel, but is compatible with much of the evidence.

**Religious morality**
I am only too aware that that leaves many questions unanswered, and it seems like a complicated yet over-simple way of thinking about morality. It was much simpler to think in terms of absolute standards set out as a set of principles and precepts. I am not advocating that we reject the morality we have used so far, but there are some ways in which the bases must be amended.

First, it used to be thought that humans are intrinsically evil, and that they need religion to be brought back into the fold. Although the doctrine of original sin is now discarded by most Christians, the idea that humans, or at least 'other people', are likely to be evil continues in part because, as we have seen, the media report muggings, murders, rapes and so on, and rarely mention any of the many kind actions that most of us encounter every day. This predilection for news about the bad requires a functional explanation: an entirely speculative answer is that it is in our interests to be on the lookout for actions or individuals who might upset the balance between prosociality and selfish assertiveness in our group; and that greater danger lies in the selfish assertiveness than in the prosociality of individuals. But if we were always on the lookout for evil, we would certainly find it, and we would act towards others as though we mistrusted them and thereby encourage their deviousness. So here again there must be a balance, in this case between expectations for prosociality and antisociality.

Second, we have seen that the evolution of morality and its development in individuals can be understood in terms of known processes of biological evolution and psychological development. Understanding that our morality has not been imposed by a deity but is something that has been created by humans so that they can live in harmonious societies will make it accessible and acceptable to many twenty-first century minds who doubt any form of theism.

Third, religious belief must not be seen as having priority over humanism in the life of the society. In a state that contains citizens from many cultural traditions and religious faiths, there is no longer any justification for one religion being specified as the state religion. There are of course understandable reasons why that has come about, and the forces of antidisestablishmentarianism are strong, but they should no longer carry overpowering weight. Some revisions in traditional ceremony are (perhaps sadly) necessary, but they would be in the interests of cultural unity. One cannot expect people of integrity, brought up in one religious tradition, readily to switch allegiance to another. We expect all citizens to have common *moral values*, but not necessarily a common belief system. What is important for societal well-being is a high degree of moral uniformity, where morality does not depend upon religious beliefs (chapter 3). Perhaps allegiance to common moral principles could be incorporated into our ceremonial instead of the more fanciful religious myths, though that would involve considerable ceremonial loss.

Fourth, for religions represented in authoritarian regimes, special problems may arise. In China the state claims control of the Church, and this has led to conflict with the Vatican: state-appointed bishops have not been recognised by the Pope. China's 10 million Catholics must chose between devotion to the Pope or to state authorities.

However, even for those who do not accept a religious doctrine, some components of religion, like religious ritual or religious music, may facilitate prosocial behaviour and/or peace of mind. This may be a continuing consequence of the way in which religiosity has been part of, and indeed central to, our culture. I have therefore suggested (Chapter 4) that our attitude to religion should be carefully selective: the anti-theists are wrong if they want to dismiss it all now, though it is possible that a time may come when that would be appropriate. As we have seen, religious belief must certainly not be seen as validating morality by association or vice versa.

This does not mean that a religious perspective has nothing to contribute to morality. We have seen that religiosity can have positive consequences for some as well as harm for others. Papal pronouncements reach an enormous audience and Pope Benedict XVI's encyclical calling for global economy oriented towards achieving the common good rather than total wealth is important for us all, though the difficulty is knowing (and agreeing) how to achieve it (O'Keefe, 1996). On the other hand, the apparently ambivalent attitude of a previous Pope to Nazism was deplorable, the Catholic ban on contraception has had very adverse consequences on the global problem of over-population, and the mass fundamentalist religions tend to trade on individual salvation rather than the common good. Religion can too easily be misused: when Lloyd Blankfein, the head of a major bank, explains away the excessive profits and bonuses of bankers by describing himself as 'doing God's work', something is clearly amiss.

**Summary**
The nature of our morality depends on our world-view. Any shift in moral values will require a shift in our perceptions of each other and of the nature of our society. Morality must be *seen* as absolute, but nevertheless have some flexibility to cope with changes in society. Some conflict is inevitable and controls will always be necessary, but they must come from within the community and not from outside entities: the righteous indignation or approval of our fellows could control our behaviour appropriately and understandably, with no need, for example, of Heaven and Hell. We need a morality that ensures that more value be placed on the well-being of the community relative to the self. Moral values must be seen as immutable, yet retain limited flexibility to cope with changes in society. The distinction between good and bad cannot be easily encapsulated in a few values or principles: in general, actions intended to improve the well-being of our fellows are good, while those that improve our own well-being but not that of others are bad.

# Part IV
# Areas for Change

Societies foster the development of institutions that are seen as serving a purpose in the society as a whole, but can cause those involved to behave in ways that, in another context, would be seen as immoral. By an institution I mean an organisation constituted to achieve one or more goals and containing a number of roles, the incumbents of each role having specified rights and duties (Hinde, 2007). One of the most important is the marketplace.

Chapter 7

# The Marketplace

## Competition

Early in human history resources were usually limited, so looking after one's own interests has usually meant that individuals competed with each other, and in most competitions someone must lose. Thus competition, though beloved by right-wing governments, can rarely be good for everyone. In the western world competitiveness seems to have become increasingly intense, partly because a trend towards hierarchical societies has meant that those at the top could corner more than their fair shares, and partly because individuals confuse *wanting* with *needing*. In recent centuries, production potential has outstripped consumption, permitting the excess to be used to enhance production still further and to create more things for people to want that are not needed. In the modern world, most economists have argued that competition among both producers and retailers brings cheaper goods to the consumer, encourages innovation, and is the mainspring of capitalism. Are they correct?

On general grounds, many would agree with them: the competitive games that play such an important and natural role in our society, and in the environment of children, are an essential element in most societies. But in such cases the attitudes of the parties involved are quite different from those to be found in the marketplace. There is also a negative side. In situations comparable to the marketplace, as human populations increase, we are approaching a situation in which the effects of competition are not only devastating for the losers but also threatening the existence of humankind. It is leading to a situation where the global environment is being changed, pollution is increasing, some of the earth's resources are becoming exhausted, animal and plant species are becoming extinct. Furthermore, excessive competition can lead to bending the rules to further one's own interests, and to corruption (Hinde, 2007).

Thus, whether or not competition brings some benefits to the community, it also brings many problems. Can the intensity of competition be reduced and its negative effects ameliorated? More importantly, can its influence outside the marketplace be confined? Can the vast discrepancies in wealth in our societies that are responsible for so much suffering (pp. 78-80) and result from competitive greed, be reduced? Can the institutions that we have created in our societies, apparently for the 'general' good, be tamed? We shall see that the incumbents of positions in those institutions can become governed by their duty to the particular institution in which they work, but yet in doing so must live in a moral world that is often at variance with their everyday life.

Capitalism must not be allowed to justify any sort of behaviour. If excessive competition has undesirable consequences, but is an inevitable result of human nature, some competition is likely always to be with us: individuals who lacked all selfish assertiveness would be little more than cabbages, with disastrous effects on the nature of society. However, we now know a little about how to provide developmental circumstances that will reduce the priority at present given to selfish assertiveness in the moral balance.

**Competition and capitalism**
Our present society is based largely on 'getting on', 'getting a good job', 'succeeding'. Selfish assertiveness takes precedence over prosociality. The game is played out in the marketplace.

Take, for example, that part of the marketplace concerned with the sale of used cars and consider the simplest possible case, the sale of a car to a buyer who needs it to get to his work. The value of a used car cannot be precisely determined, but can be specified only in terms of what buyers are prepared to pay and what sellers are prepared to receive in exchange. If there is to be any point to a deal, the buyer must value the car more than the seller. If the buyer would be willing to pay up to £500, but offers £350, and the seller is willing to let it go for £400 but tries to get more, they are likely to bargain, and ultimately agree on around £450. Both are then satisfied: the buyer gets the car for less than he would have been willing to pay and the seller gets more than he would have sold it for (Hinde, 2007).

In the real world, each is striving to get the best deal he can, and knows that the other is similarly motivated. The seller will try to get more than £400, and the buyer will try to pay less than £500. In bargaining the seller will extol the merits of the car, the buyer will call attention to the rust on the door. Each tries to get the best for himself, and knows the other is doing the same. In terms of the Golden Rule, neither is doing to the other as he would like to be done by. And yet both knew the rules and accepted the situation. The buyer recognised that, in the business world, the seller must try to make a profit, and the seller recognised that the buyer must husband his resources. It is intrinsic to the nature of the marketplace that sellers try to get the best price that they can and buyers pay as little as they can get away with. At the simplest level in which one individual is selling an object to another it is just accepted that both seller and buyer understand the game and will drive as hard a bargain as they can; the Golden Rule is inverted to I-am-going-to-get-as-much-as-I-can-out-of-you-because-I-know-you-are-trying-to-get-as-much-as-you-can-out-of-me, and each suspects the other of being conservative with the truth. (There is an interesting cultural difference here. In the West there is a feeling that there is something slightly tainted about bargaining, whereas in many Middle Eastern countries bargaining is a matter of honour: a seller or buyer who does less well than he could have is seen to be weak).

Most marketplaces have numerous buyers and sellers, and the 'fair' price may be influenced by the bargains already concluded. If one seller has sold an object for £450, other sellers are unlikely to get more from another buyer for a similar object, and may be forced to accept less. Thus competition between buyers to get the object for as little as possible will tend to keep prices low for all consumers. The nature of the marketplace provides excuses for abandoning the everyday morality that sees 'fairness' as a desirable goal. Although economists have argued that what we see as immoral at the individual level can benefit the collective, it is inescapable that the nature of the marketplace provides excuses for abandoning the everyday morality that sees 'fairness' as a desirable goal.

It is easy to see how the problems multiply in larger business enterprises. At the more complicated level of the company, the Chief Executive Officer may feel that his principal duty is to maximise the dividend of shareholders, but he is placed in the impossible position of having to satisfy a number of different stakeholders, for he also has duties to the workforce, the customers, his suppliers and others according to the nature of the business. The inversion of the Golden Rule may be seen to be 'justified' to some extent by the need to please the buyer or shareholders and is seen as proper policy for guiding business dealings in many contexts. However, the recent trend in the USA away from this stakeholder view to one dominated by profit and shareholder maximisation may not be in the interest of the country as a whole (Gomory & Sylla, 2013; Dasgupta, pers. comm.).

Inevitably, the consequences of competition ramify throughout society. Each manufacturer tries to make sure that more of his products are sold than those of other manufacturers. Retailers add their efforts to the same end. One consequence of this marketplace competitiveness has been excessive consumerism in all branches of society. We are persuaded to buy more than we need, we buy objects that we will never use, we have to have not just the best and the newest, but something better and more up-to-date than our neighbour's. The belief that the price of an object is 'reduced' is a powerful incentive to buy it, whether or not one needs it. This is in part the result of the manufacturers and retail merchants trying to sell as many of their products as they can. They know how to take advantage of human selfish assertiveness to sell their wares, and must carry some responsibility for the greed that can lead to shoppers being trampled underfoot when the doors open for the January sales; for the inability of people to discriminate between what is necessary and what it would be nice to have; for the power of the credit system enabling customers to buy now and pay later; and for making goods that will soon need to be replaced. When people are in the marketplace, it may be to the detriment of their personal relationships and of other aspects of their lives.

Discussion about competition at the company level often neglects the fact that competition inevitably involves a loser as well as a winner. It may lead to putting a rival firm out of business, with resulting unemployment. Economists have maintained that competition is an essential part of the business world and is to be encouraged: as a result the businessman (or woman) can see his behaviour as guided by an ethic that justifies selfish assertiveness not only on the grounds that the same precept applies to all those involved, but also that the public is better served. It is easy to forget that *'A highly dynamic capitalist economy.....is necessarily continually creating new products, while seeking to produce established ones more profitably. This creativity in the pursuit of profit necessitates destroying the value of older products and the skills, companies and livelihoods of those involved in producing them'* (Szreter, 2010). This effect could be ameliorated by sympathy for the losers as suggested originally by Adam Smith (Fehr & Fischbacker, 2003; Richerson, personal communication), but the extent to which sympathy operates in the competitive and global world is not large. CEOs have so many responsibilities to shareholders and suppliers that they can have little room for sympathies for competitors on whose failure their own success depends.

Competition in the marketplace must, however, have some regulation. The positive effects of competition in lowering prices for the consumer could be lost if there were no limits. In practice there are limits on collusion between firms, price-fixing, inadequate bookkeeping and so on. One unfortunate consequence of such laws is that they enable those playing the competition game to feel they are playing by the rules and thus less inclined to bridle their competitiveness.

Competition also influences life inside the company. The employees are likely to compare the pay they get with that of others. What is fair? What matters in real life is whether each member of every dyad considers the situation to be fair, not whether it is actually so. Do the employees see themselves as a group? Any one who calls in sick will be putting a greater load on the others. Do they support him for getting one up on the management? Do they support him so long as he does not skive off too often? Or do they expose him? In the workplace, Homans (1961, 1974) argued that individuals, in seeking for 'fairness', expect rewards in relation to their costs. His work led to the family of 'exchange theories' (see pp. 38-40), but many studies have shown the complexity and situation-dependence of the concept of fairness (Asma, 2013).

At the governmental level, it must not be assumed that competitive capitalism is a god whose dictates must be followed at all costs, nor must it be assumed that increasing competition will automatically increase efficiency and the well-being of all concerned. British Railways was split into local companies in the belief that competitive bidding for the franchises would reduce prices and increase efficiency. From the passenger's point of view the result has been in many respects a reduction in efficiency. For instance, a train journey in the UK may require two or three tickets from separate companies for a single journey. If the train on one line is late so that a connection is missed, it is unlikely that either company will accept responsibility. And only rarely does the passenger have choice of carriers. The British National Health Service, something citizens have been proud of for decades, is being slowly destroyed by a government's insistence on the introduction of a marketplace mentality, thereby belittling the dedication of its employees. In the Law, there has been a tendency towards competitive tendering for legal aid with contracts going to the lowest bidder. As a result, young, poorly paid and inexperienced lawyers could be given cases for which they are not yet ready and the client is poorly served (H. Kennedy, personal communication). And the UK Government recently privatised the Royal Mail, another institution of which employees and customers are justly proud. Employee motivation gets left out of market calculations.

I have already mentioned another aspect to this: the earth's resources are not unlimited, consumerism leads to depletion of rare minerals and other valuable materials and to pollution of the atmosphere and the resulting climatic changes. Frugality is imperative today. If India and China were to have the same number of cars per person as western countries, global warming would be even more disastrous than it is now.

**Inequalities**
Competitiveness must play a part in the growing gap between rich and poor. So long as we had the erroneous Reagan/Thatcher view that wealth would trickle down to the less well-off, the trend for that gap to widen in practice seemed inescapable: it is easier for the haves to earn more than the have-nots in both absolute and relative terms, and the gap inevitably widens. The differences between rich and poor are related to many factors in the structure of society, differ between societies and change with time: all this has been carefully documented by Piketty (2013). Ultimately, however, the wealth differences stem largely from greed and good fortune on one side and from lack of opportunity and bad luck on the other. Markets are said to provide the buyer with freedom of choice, but what a person chooses is inevitably influenced by the size of his purse. And, as we shall see, inequality has many consequences on health and prospects.

Piketty's analysis focuses on the nature and the factors affecting inequalities. The extent of these inequalities has varied with time and place. For instance, the share of the top 10% of the population (i.e the so-called upper class) in the total income (from labour and capital) has varied from 25% in Scandinavia in the 1970s-1980s to 50+% in Europe and the USA in 1910. The wealth difference between the richer citizens and the poorer ones fell during the twentieth century, apparently primarily as a consequence of the two world wars and the great depression, together with governmental policies of rent control and taxation. Now, the difference appears to be increasing again. '*When rate of return on capital significantly exceeds the growth rate of the economy ... then it logically follows that inherited wealth grows faster than output and income. People with inherited wealth need save only a portion of their income from capital to see that capital grow more quickly than the economy as a whole.*'

At another level of analysis, other factors contribute to the wealth gap. For instance, middle and upper class parents resent inheritance tax on the ground that striving to give one's children a good start is a powerful incentive, and that it is their right to do what they like with their assets. But it is clearly unfair that other children should be handicapped by the bad luck of having been born into a poor family. And it seems very difficult for the education system to make sure the situation is not perpetuated. Working class homes tend to have fewer books, to have fewer family discussions, and to lack quiet space for study at home as compared with middle class homes. Some working class parents may encourage children to leave school to get a job and augment the family income rather than facilitating their children's further study with a view to a more satisfying job or entry to university.

The situation is exacerbated by the media. In catering to public taste they feed it. By focusing on the rich and famous, the celebrity culture encourages the growth of materialism and can lead to a steady deterioration in society. The focus is on *things*: the value that many have placed on finding meaning in their lives, a meaning that comes from living in a just world, goes by the board.

We all want to acquire the things we need. It is part of our nature. But capitalism encourages excessive striving for material goods that we do not need. Advertising, an inevitable adjunct to competition, leads to consumerism. Increasingly, anyone without a personal computer, mobile phone or comparable device cannot communicate adequately (that is by current standards) with his peers. Whether or not that is a good thing is an open issue, but it feeds the competitive urge. The competitive urge to have more is never satisfied: it leads to wanting more, and more and more yet again. We must have more and better than the next man.

Competition inevitably leads to inequality. Inequality, as it exists in most western societies, cannot be desirable. Given that Christian doctrine was first formulated and disseminated with the aim of winning converts amongst an underclass whose chances of bettering their situation by open revolt were extremely slender, it is not surprising that acceptance of the status quo was an important part of its message. 'Blessed are the meek …'. But how should that translate in the modern capitalist world? Accepting the present situation without modification cannot lead to a better world.

There is extensive evidence, both within countries and across countries, and by many indices of well-being, that income inequality is associated with social disadvantage. In their review of the need for greater equality, Wilkinson and Pickett (2009) demonstrate in developed countries a close relation between income inequality and increasing mental illness, drug use, obesity, teenage pregnancy, violence and infant mortality, and decreasing life expectancy, educational achievement and social mobility. Some of the richer countries actually do worse overall than the poorer countries, implying that inferior material conditions are not the sole issue: rather, it is the inequality within society that is basic. Indeed we should probably go further than that: it is not so much inequality itself but the perception of inequality that is the issue (see below).

Wealth differentials also lead to inefficiency. The difference between the highest and the lowest incomes within society or within firms has been increasing rapidly in recent years: as a result of the increase in income differences, some employees feel their pay rates are unfair and this harms the organisation's effectiveness. Top salaries in the UK are now approaching a million UK pounds a year, in some cases much more. The basic pay of a Chief Executive Officer in one of the major firms is now over 80 times the average worker's salary (Hutton, 2010). The rewards obtained by the highest paid are just simply too great. Why should anyone need so much? It is not only that it is so easy for those involved to fail to recognise when enough is enough, but that those who gain most are not those who have contributed most.

Life expectancy increases with economic development (gross national income per head) amongst the poorer countries, but not amongst the richer ones. Amongst the latter it is the *differences* between rich and poor that are crucial. With increasing income inequality, health and social problems increase. The crucial issue seems to be the differences in status that are associated with the income differences. Strong evidence shows that there has been an increase in anxiety and depression in the USA since the nineteen fifties. This, surprisingly, was associated with an apparent increase in self-esteem. However, this overall picture of increasing self-esteem has been due to two quite different effects: in one group the increase in self-esteem was associated with happiness, confidence, an ability to make friends and so on, but there was also a second group who scored high on self-esteem but tended to racism, violence and insensitivity in personal relationships. In this second group the self-esteem involved a denial of weakness and an attempt to maintain a positive sense of self in the face of imagined criticism (Wilkinson & Pickett, 2009). It seems that the increase in anxiety is a consequence of increasing social stress and an inability of individuals to feel at ease with each other.

Interviewing high earning lawyers and bankers, Toynbee and Walker (2008) found that those with the higher incomes were extraordinarily ignorant about what other people earn, tending to overestimate the incomes of their poorer contemporaries, as though diminishing the unfairness of their own position and trying to emphasise their own ordinariness. Toynbee and Walker (p. 36) comment *'Here are people (the higher earners) who may be technically adept, or good at deal-making, but as a group with one or two exceptions – they were less intelligent, less intellectually inquisitive, less knowledgeable and, despite their good schools, less broadly educated than high flyers in other profession ... Their high salaries were not a sign of any obvious superiority'*. In our increasingly undemocratic society the income differential is self-perpetuating: rich parents mean better schooling, a better start in adult life and subsequent earning power, while poverty leads to poorer qualifications, worse jobs and poorer health. Furthermore, in Britain the situation is exacerbated by the complex devices that the rich alone can use to avoid paying all the taxes that are due.

The bottom line is that the competitiveness encouraged by the marketplace enhances the self-assertiveness that almost requires dishonesty and leads to inequality in wealth, excessive consumerism, waste and inefficiency.

## Poverty

Poverty can be defined in many ways, and a tight definition is difficult to find. This is in part because it is a relative matter: the European Community has used the following definition:

*People are said to be living in poverty if their income and resources are so inadequate as to preclude them from having a standard of living considered acceptable in the society in which they live. Because of their poverty they may experience multiple disadvantage through unemployment, low income, poor housing, inadequate health care and barriers to lifelong learning, culture, sport and recreation. They are often excluded and marginalised from participating in activities (economic, social and cultural) that are the norm for other people and their access to fundamental rights may be restricted.*

Social scientists who need to measure the incidence of poverty quantitatively may compare each household's income with the median (middle) income in the society, defining those with an income less than 60% of the median as 'poor'. But such a measure is misleading if used across a range of societies. According to the Food and Agricultural Organisation, 870 million people do not have enough to eat, and 98% of these live in developing countries. A household classed as poor in Europe might still be far from starvation. In any case, individuals are especially sensitive to the difference between their own income and that of others in their societies. In the USA the ratio of the average compensation received by CEOs to the average received by production workers has risen dramatically in recent years: one source indicates from around 30:1 to over 200:1 in the nearly fifty years since 1966.

I do not wish to imply that financial wealth is all that matters, far from it. The EC definition of poverty, cited above, implies that many other issues are also involved, though many of them are related to financial resources. Social scientists are trying out different measures of 'happiness' but there is as yet no general agreement. The trouble is that we are living in a market-oriented society that purveys precisely the message that money brings happiness.

**Taming business competition**
Given the perceptions of Adam Smith, it is not surprising that competition is the driving force in the business world. It is likely that it will remain so. The important issue is, can it be tamed sufficiently for its adverse affects to be ameliorated?

The question of monitoring commercial competition between companies is an urgent matter for economists (Stiglitz, 2006). Some progress has been made in the regulation of corporations and false accounting has led to gaol sentences. It helps if a firm's officers are personally responsible for the decisions they make and if firms and/or their officers can be made to pay for damage done. Firms should be responsible to all stakeholders, so that it should be seen as proper for environmental considerations to lead to a reduction in shareholders' dividends. Regulations about the quality of goods and against built-in obsolescence might be possible, but very difficult to enforce. But these are all top-down matters and beyond the scope of this book (Figure 1).

What is required is a change in world-views over the whole social scale – managers, workers and individual consumers. At present we accept that those who deal in a marketplace act on the basis that others are greedy, that the marketplace has its own rules, and turn a blind eye to differences from the morality of the outside world. That perpetuates the situation. We have a market economy, but economists are only slowly realising that people are not wholly greedy; Dasgupta, personal communication). Many, perhaps most, people prefer dealings to be fair – though what counts as fair is not always clear: as noted above, 'fairness' poses difficult problems. Economists argue that rewards should be proportional to work put in and the risks taken (Hutton, 2010) and the market would probably work better that way. But some allowance must be made for the sick, the handicapped, the aged, and the consequences of bad and good luck. Lady Luck may try to distribute her favours equally, but it is the needy who get the short straws.

Encouraging fair dealing may be a matter of self-interest, if only those involved would see it: if an ethic of fair dealing prevails now, I shall not have to worry so much when I next enter the market. But the nature of the market encourages deceit and greed. The gross unfairness in the incomes of bankers, derived from gambling with other people's money without responsibility when they lose, has become public knowledge and a matter of public protest since the 2008 recession. Money changes hands, but the community is not better off. Clearly, the banks must be controlled effectively, but can a government take that on successfully? It is possible for a financier to become unbelievably rich while convincing himself that he has not broken any of the moral rules of our society. This is partly the result of the role of institutions in our society, discussed above. But it also requires focussing on the consequences for others of what one does rather than solely on its consequences for oneself. In the end, if some get richer, it is highly likely that others will get poorer.

**Employee ownership**
The effects of competition between employees within firms or businesses can be ameliorated in firms that are owned by the employees and are organised as cooperatives/commonwealths, such as Scott Bader and John Lewis. Employees who have a feeling of autonomy because they have a degree of control over their work are least affected by income differentials. Especially beneficial are cooperative enterprises where the employees own the company and participate in its management. The John Lewis Partnership and the Scott Bader Commonwealth are shining examples of this principle. In Scott Bader Commonwealth Ltd., management is not responsible to external

shareholders, and decisions on the proportion of profits to be put back into the company is in the hands of the workers, or their representatives, themselves. Employee ownership produces a sense of responsibility towards the organisation and, hopefully, to society as a whole. In such enterprises the workers are likely to agree that, in view of the responsibility carried, the executives should be paid more than the workers, but not dozens or hundreds of times more. The membership decides on rates of pay and on the ratio between the highest and lowest (recently 14:1 in Scott Bader). There is evidence that, by various measures of well-being, the influence of such companies spreads into the wider community. It is of interest that the principle of cooperative ownership was endorsed in 1961 and 1981 by the Pope, who also exhorted the Roman Catholic Church to cease supporting the more powerful elements in society (O'Keefe, 1996).

Unfortunately competition is becoming more and more dominant in society and seems to be taking charge of our lives. In sport competitiveness is enhanced by the excessive financial consequences of winning. General knowledge competitions on the television may be accompanied by derision for the losers, and the competitions are nearly always competitions for money.

**Summary**
Our society depends on institutions that we have devised for our own good, but which can destroy morality because people are required to judge actions by criteria other than those used in ordinary life. The most powerful is the marketplace. The Golden Rule of do-as-you-would-be-done-by is abandoned in favour of I-am-going-to-get-the-best-I-can-out-of-you-because-I-know-you-are-going-to-try-to-get-the-best-you-can-out-of-me. Although economists have thought the marketplace is a force for good because it keeps prices low for consumers, and although it is part of our nature to look after our own interests, competitiveness is entering every facet of our lives. Present inequalities are responsible for many of society's ills. Competitiveness cannot be eliminated but must be tamed.

Chapter 8
# Some Other Institutions

In the preceding chapter we discussed the institution of the marketplace where, in the simplest case, buyer and seller must agree on a price and stick to the agreement. The marketplace has spawned other institutions that facilitate their own functioning, like parts of the law: individuals may be deterred from reneging on agreements by fear of legal retribution. The law itself is an institution with many constituent roles – judge, jury and so on (Hinde, 2006). Beyond that, societies create conventions concerning what is or is not proper behaviour – conventions to which citizens are expected to conform. The marketplace could function only if incumbents of its roles conformed to the conventions of the society, often seen as commonly recognised principles of morality, as well as the requirements of the law. In other words, individuals must trust each other, and have the ability to deter those who offend the conventions without bringing in the often cumbersome machinery of the law.

In this chapter we consider some other institutions in which the behaviour of individuals occupying certain roles may contravene the requirements of societal morality (Hinde, 2007).

## Politics

The democratic system itself contains many moral traps, some almost unavoidable. If democracy is to work, voters must believe that their elected representatives have their interests at heart, and not their own. In presenting him/herself to the electorate a candidate must usually show himself to be a loyal member of a political party and tailor his own views to those he believes to be held by the electorate and especially that section of the electorate likely to be important for his election. To some extent he/she must disguise his real opinions.

In the UK Parliament, and the US Congress, the elected members' views may be swayed by unelected lobbyists, often richly endowed by commercial interests. And party politics sometimes constrains how they vote in debates. The 'Whip' may require them to vote according to the wishes of the leader of their party, thereby placing the elected members in a conflict between loyalty to their own party, their own ambitions and their own integrity. The party has helped in their election, and loyalty to the party may be seen as a moral obligation. If they do not vote in line with the leader's wishes, they may lose their chances of preferment or suffer exclusion from the party. Thus the party system may involve both carrot and stick for the elected members. One wonders how far party loyalty is essential, and whether the Whip system could be diluted? Why cannot lobbyists' attempts improperly to influence policies and the voting of individual members be curtailed?

Elected individuals, of course, may be tempted to put their own interests first, so that voting for reforms that are believed to be in the nation's interests but against those of the individual politician requires considerable integrity. A government's ability to contribute to the solution of world problems is severely handicapped by its need to please its voters: the failure of the USA to ratify the Kyoto Protocol on climate change because it was claimed that it would harm the US economy disregarded the longer-term view that not ratifying it could harm their children and grandchildren.

Adam Smith argued that self-interest was proper in the marketplace, but not in politics. I have argued that there are limits on the propriety of self-interest in the marketplace (chapter 7) and the case is even stronger for politics. Those who rule must put the common good above their own and consider themselves bound by the laws that bind the electorate. This makes democracy inevitably fragile so that constant vigilance is necessary. A politician's life may be his own, but integrity in all matters related to his work is essential and transparency is necessary.

However, the problem does not lie only with the politicians. The voting public must be attuned to its responsibilities, including the responsibility to vote in elections. It has been argued that a democracy, to be successful and to ensure the involvement of its members, must embrace groups that practise 'direct democracy', where all the members of the group vote on every issue. It would be nearly impossible for all citizens in a parliamentary democracy in a large state to vote on every issue, but the existence of smaller community-based groups where individuals in the group could practise direct voting may enhance responsibility to vote in parliamentary elections. Direct democracy could facilitate a sense of community involving friendships that creates trust between individuals and makes it possible for individuals to accept differences of opinion and compromises. The existence of smaller groups within the society that help to build up 'social capital' does in fact benefit the well-being of the citizens (Putnam, 2000).

Democracy in a complex society involves the election of representatives by the electorate, and then as a result of further votes, an overall leader. This system may result in the Party Leader being put under great stress. For every decision he (she) must weigh up the consequences of every possible action, the views of colleagues and the Opposition, and often also of Third Parties. He may have to make momentous decisions with inadequate information when he is physically exhausted. His own views may be contrary to those of the majority of the electorate: should he follow the public or try to lead them? Such issues became particularly acute in the lead-up to the Second Gulf War (Hinde, 2007).

I have chosen examples from national and international politics, but similar problems must be faced at every level down to the Parish Council, and in every supposedly democratic committee that regulates our affairs. Although democracy is the best system available, it leads to situations where democratic principles may be far from straightforward. Integrity in elected members is essential.

**War**
War can be seen as an institution: in preparations for war, or in war itself, the behaviour of individuals is largely governed by the duties associated with the roles they occupy in the institution of war. Not only do the combatants fight in part because it is their duty to fight, but the workers in armament factories, the commanders, the politicians, the medics do what they do in part because of the duties associated with their roles in the institution of war.

Many have believed that war is an inevitable consequence of the human condition. That is a mistake (Hinde & Rotblat, 2003). In time, people will recognise that, in modern war, both sides lose. In addition, war is immoral, wasteful, and cruel. International disputes are better settled around the conference table, not with guns, for violence only breeds more violence. I do not deny that, in today's world, war may sometimes, though very rarely, be necessary, but it can legally be started only by, or on behalf of, the United Nations (UN Charter, Articles 2:3 and 2:4). Unfortunately, the United Nations, like its predecessor the League of Nations, is prevented by its Charter from interfering in conflicts within states, and has neither the power nor the structure to be effective in preventing or ameliorating inter-state conflicts. Its lack of resources is another example of selfish individualism at another level of complexity: when it comes to votes on the Security Council or General Assembly countries tend to look after their own interests and the needs of the world are forgotten.

The evolutionary forces shown in Figure 2 illustrate the difficulty of solving conflicts between groups. Towards fellow members of our own group we have propensities both for prosocial and selfishly assertive behaviour. Towards outsiders we have mainly the latter. Here, it may be suggested, lies the importance of personal meetings between the leaders of opposing groups. They are most likely to find common ground if, first, they discuss common personal problems – their families or children or recreational preferences, perhaps. The understanding of each other as individuals, having a common humanity, can then ease the way towards solving the political issues.

If we are to hasten the day when war is abolished or at least seen as a very last resort, we must work at two levels, the political level, from the top downwards, and with the grass roots, from the bottom up. In democracies, efforts can be made to influence politicians, to provide them with accurate information on the probable consequences of their decisions, and to act as a go-between in disputes: the International Pugwash organisation, the UK Pugwash Group and other NGOs have had considerable success in this way. Their work depends on maintaining a reputation for impeccable scientific integrity and lack of bias.

With the general public, a variety of approaches are possible: in Britain the UK Pugwash Group, the Movement for the Abolition of War, the Campaign for Nuclear Disarmament and other organisations do dedicated work. The task is becoming increasingly difficult as the proportion of people with first-hand experience of war decreases, so convincing the young of its real nature is of special importance (Hinde & Rotblat, 2003; Marlantes, 2011).

The pictures of the horrors of war that appear almost every day in the media tend to deaden the emotions so that the suffering intrinsic to war becomes almost a commonplace. Perhaps the most moving are the accounts given by survivors, especially by those who saw their experiences in retrospect in a different light from their view at the time. For instance, Peter Johnson, an RAF bomber pilot in World War II, initially saw the bombing of German cities as part of his role as a bomber pilot: *'What we had to do was search for the coloured lights dropped by our own people, aim our bombs at them and get away.'* In time, as lead aircraft in an attack on a small German town, he knew civilian *'casualties were bound to be high because the roofs of cellars and shelters would collapse'* but felt that he must go ahead as he had been ordered. Later, he came to realise the horrific truth of what his bombs were doing on the ground, and became sure *'that what we were to do was not only wrong but stupid'*. After the war he bitterly regretted his part in it (Johnson, 1995).

Another example, reported in the newspapers 60 years after the event, was a German machine gunner defending Omaha Beach as the Americans landed, who believed that he had killed 2,000 soldiers at long range as they landed looking to him *'like ants'*. But it was not that that gave him nightmares after the war: it was the moment when he shot a young American who came running up the beach closer to him. It was the memory of his contorted face that made him realise he had been killing people all the time.

In addition, working at both the political and the man-in-the-street levels could be greatly facilitated by an understanding of what motivates individuals on the other side. This has been the province of the intelligence services, but they are primarily concerned with thwarting the enemy's plans. In the new style of war with suicide bombers and improvised explosive devices, the understanding of what motivates individual bombers, and especially the influence of their religion, may be of great value (Atran, 2010).

## Churches

Adherents to some religions have regarded it as blasphemous and a deadly sin to criticise their religious beliefs. Even in my more tolerant society an atheistically inclined agnostic like myself finds it difficult to say all that he might about the church's public attitudes to religious stories for fear of offending. But to such an outsider it seems that church leaders are required to purvey as truth myths that it is difficult to believe they hold themselves. What is meant by 'I believe' has somewhat nebulous boundaries: it seems improbable to me that the church can do itself much good by treating unverifiable and extremely improbable myths as true records of happenings in the material world. Yet they have been expected to present them as the truth to a less educated public.

Some churches have imposed on their own officials moral standards that many are unable to meet, but the religious authorities are clearly aware of their own internal problems and it is unnecessary to comment here.

## Summary

Whereas the marketplace is an especially important example of an institution that causes us to behave according to moral standards at odds with those used in our everyday lives, there are many others. Here, politics, war, and religion are considered.

Chapter 9

# Personal and Group Relations

In the last two chapters we have considered the role of certain institutions in undermining morality in society. Here we consider some other factors in modern societies that need special attention.

**Population growth**
Excessive competition and many of its ills could be ameliorated if the number of consumers were controlled. The world's population has been growing exponentially and apparently inexorably in recent decades, standing at around 7 billion at present and predicted to be about 10 billion by 2050. We are approaching a situation in which the world can no longer bear the crushing load of people trampling on its surface. Our survival depends on our environment, but we are making demands on it that cannot continue to be met. Already human activities are producing climate change, and many species of plant and animal have become extinct. And extinct means for always, for ever and ever: science has no magic wand with which to reverse the effects of man's greed. We are changing the world, making it less and less habitable for ourselves. We know we are doing it, but we are too selfish, greedy or lazy to do much about it (www.populationmatters.org). It is not enough merely to lament the trend: we need a better understanding of the dynamics of the mutual relations between population size, consumption and the environment (Dasgupta & Ehrlich, 2013).

The forces behind population growth are clear enough and do not need elaboration here. Biologically, sex is one of the most powerful motivators. Culturally, in many and perhaps most societies, kudos is attached to having a large family: more bread-winners, more relatives to ensure your safe passage into the next life. Governments seem powerless in attempts to control what is seen as an expression of individual freedom. Religious prohibitions from the Roman Catholic Church, though now losing their potency, have been placed on any form of birth control. Though limitation of family size has been imposed in China, it has been more successful in towns than in the countryside, and it is having undesirable demographic consequences by biasing the birth ratio towards boys. And, contributing still further to population growth, death rates have been decreasing through better living conditions, better sanitation, more adequate supplies of clean drinking water, and advances in medical science – all measures to be pursued as decreasing suffering, but measures that must be accompanied by education and help with birth control.

We understand many of the issues that are leading to population growth, but our efforts to use that knowledge have been largely unsuccessful. A major factor has been that any attempt to control population runs against cultural beliefs and deeply embedded worldviews. It is there we must seek for change, asking what the consequences to the community would be if every couple had three children?

**Urban living**
A major proportion of the world's population now lives in cities, where children grow up in conditions very different from those experienced by most children only a few hundred years ago. Urban living has become the norm for most people largely because the opportunities are greater in the towns than in the countryside, it is the way to 'get on'. As a result, citizens meet everyday many people whom they do not know as individuals. This may have profound effects, both positive and negative, on psychological, physiological, physical and moral development. Among the positive effects are ease of communication and greater access to literacy, especially for women; access to start-up capital; access to advocacy groups in support of rights to housing, work, etc.; exposure to a wider range of cultures, beliefs, etc. sometimes leading to increased tolerance; and greater access to health facilities and to public transport. The negative effects are largely the reverse: the prevalence of misinformation, isolation within a mass of anonymous individuals, segregation, dislocation of family and personal relationships, and greater exposure to epidemics.

More important in the present context, the incentives of urban living can cause the balance between selfish assertiveness and prosociality to swing beyond our individual psychological capacities to control it. 'Having' has become more important than 'being'; unbridled competitiveness is too often seen as a prime virtue. Connections to families, friends and groups have become more tortuous and remote as we make our own way in the world and, in the west (see pp. 100-102), society has become more individual-oriented. With dense urbanisation, children become less cooperative (Graves & Graves, 1983) and grow up with a different, more ego-oriented view of the world. To get the best out of urban living, many data suggest that we should pay more attention to social development and the development of personal relationships (see below). For life in towns to be fully successful we need both the ability to understand our fellow human beings at more than a superficial level, and we need a stronger sense of community and of responsibility for the well-being of all its members than those demanded by village life.

Violence is high in cities, but the number of people killed seems to be related not to the actual size of the city as to poverty and especially the rate of population growth. It seems that both individuals and civic institutions are slow to adapt to rapid increases in population.

There is no turning the clock back, but the problems of urban life can be ameliorated. Medical knowledge and good architectural planning have done much to ameliorate them: rickets and cholera are now much more rare in the UK than formerly and planners recognise the importance of green open spaces (see e.g. Jacobs, 1961).

**Personal relationships**
Every society is based on personal relationships between at least some of its members. The systematic study of adult personal relationships was almost totally neglected until the late twentieth century, the delay being largely due to a feeling that any science must be modelled on physics and the considerable difficulty in describing the subjective properties of relationships. Progress will not come from regarding such properties as trust, intimacy or love as intangible states that we know about 'instinctively' anyway: we must have hard-headed description and analysis to build an ordered body of knowledge. Now several journals are devoted to the study of relationships, relating them to the psychological, hormonal and neurophysiological properties of individuals as well as to cultural factors. But there is a long way to go.

As an example of the way in which psychologists have tried to come to terms with the subjective aspects of relationships, some of the recent work has focused on identifying critical properties of relationships (review, Hinde, 1997). It has become apparent that the formation of a close relationship, and falling in love, involve a change in how the participants see themselves and each other. A variety of instruments have been devised for answering such questions as 'Does A see B as similar to how A sees A?'(*i.e.* Does A see B as similar to how he sees him or herself?); 'Does A see B as similar to how B sees B?' (*i.e.* Does A understand B?) and 'Does B feel that A sees B as B sees B?' (*i.e.* Does B feel understood) (e.g. Drewery, 1969). These are of course subjective issues, and difficult to assess reliably, but they are crucial in the ability of the partners to behave prosocially to and identify with each other. Identification may involve willingness to act in a way costly to the actor but rewarding to the partner, sharing vicariously pleasure in 'doing it together' and the partner's pleasure and success (Murray & Holmes, 1996). Indeed, close relationship formation can be seen as 'including the other in the self' (Aron & Aron, 1996). Here, then, is an ability too little understood but possessed by us all and waiting to be exploited more effectively in our social lives. There are, of course, many other psychological aspects of being human that contribute to our social life, but they would take us too far from the present focus. I am certainly not wishing to belittle the work of psychiatrists and others who have been concerned with the subjective aspects of relationships, but there is clearly *also* a need for the more precise description that instruments of the sort described above provide.

Another example is provided by assessments of the quality of the attachment relationship of an infant or young child to a particular caregiver, such as mother or father. A standard laboratory situation permits analysis of how the child greets the caregiver following the stress of a brief separation. The 'attachment relationship' may be reliably coded in terms of a *dimension* of 'security of attachment' from 1 to 9, as well as a *category* of attachment reflecting the child's *pattern* of behaviour, e.g., 'secure', 'insecure-avoidant', 'insecure-ambivalent', or 'insecure-disorganised' (Parkes *et al* eds., 1991). These patterns, whose antecedents lie in the sensitive responsiveness (or not) of the caregiver, have been associated with later social development: the secure pattern is associated with well-being and consideration for others (Ainsworth, Blehar, Waters, & Wall, 1978; reviewed in Cassidy & Shaver, 2008).

By the age of about four years, most children develop a 'theory of mind', namely the ability to see oneself and others in terms of mental states – desires, emotions, beliefs, intentions – that result in human actions (e.g., Baron-Cohen, 1997; Wellman, Cross, & Watson, 2001). But we need more than that: we need mutual understanding to create close relationships and smoothly functioning groups. Mutual understanding embraces the concepts of 'interpersonal perception' and 'empathy'. Interpersonal perception involves cognitive issues, as noted above. 'Empathy' emphasises the emotional side of interpersonal perception, the extent to which individuals share the pain of another's suffering, or the joy of another's happiness. For intimate relationships we need to encourage more trust, intimacy, understanding and empathy (review, Hinde, 1997). Understanding another includes understanding his/her motives, although this could in some cases lead to hostility. Thus understanding must be coupled with an ability to act in a way conducive to reducing possible conflict.

Understanding how to enhance the quality of interpersonal relationships is perhaps the most important and the most difficult problem facing humankind, and certainly not a matter to be summarised in a few paragraphs. I will not attempt to enter further into that field, but limit myself to a statement that is something more than mere speculation. Early relationships influence the characteristics of later relationships (Bowlby, 1969, 1973, 1980). A capacity for mutual understanding probably develops as a sequel to an upbringing characterised by sensitive loving care and reasoned discipline, augmented by discussion between child and caregiver of particular situations as they arise.

There is an immediate and obvious problem. Individual self-assertiveness, doing the best for oneself, is part of human nature and can be disruptive of close relationships. Sensitive child-rearing is the most important but not the only route to ameliorating this. The goals towards which self-assertiveness is directed are widely different across societies and across individuals within societies. Some goals are common to individuals in virtually all societies, especially those goals directly connected with reproduction, and some which are indirectly but functionally connected with reproduction, such as social dominance. But goals connected with reproduction can seem to take curious forms: psychiatrists and psychoanalysts are only too ready to trace relations between sex and the goals of artistic expression and appreciation. And many find expression for their self-assertiveness in ways that can hardly be connected to reproductive goals: the willingness of many fans to queue for hours in the rain to see their favourite football team play, the passion with which the ornithologist pursues the sight of a rare bird, or the hours spent on delicate carving to get a four-masted ship into a bottle.

Since life goals are almost infinitely variable, they must be labile. We have seen that there are societies that owe their very nature to the fact that their members direct their self-assertiveness towards maintaining an egalitarian society (pp. 40-42, pp. 108-112). An egalitarian society requires individuals who see an egalitarian society as desirable for themselves and are prepared to direct their self-assertiveness to achieving it, even at some cost to themselves. That means that we must try to inculcate such an attitude in the next generation. I suggest that we must learn from the societies of hunter/gatherers described on pp. 40-42. This does not mean imitating hunter/gatherer societies, but understanding how they work and abstracting principles that would help guide our efforts to improve our own. A perfectly egalitarian society is certainly beyond our reach, and may not be desirable, but it must be given much higher priority as a goal than it gets at present.

Already we have many non-governmental organisations dedicated to improving the world, such as Greenpeace, Amnesty and Médecins sans Frontières. Such organisations depend for support primarily on individuals who work not primarily for financial gain, and therein lies hope for the future. We need to encourage small, perhaps local, groups in which every member can feel responsible for the whole (Putnam, 2000). A focus on the good of all is a proper antidote to selfishness. It is all too clear that at present our own personal interests are tending to take absolute priority over those of the community, and we need to put more emphasis on the latter than we do.

We do not need a carrot or stick external to the society for this: the approval or disapproval of peers can go a long way towards taking their place. Both mathematical modelling of society (Boyd & Richerson, 1992, 2005) and the example of modern small-scale societies (Boehm, 2012) show that a healthy respect for the good of the community requires sanctions against anti-social behaviour: there must be at least some individuals willing to punish those who display too much self-assertiveness (pp. 42-43). This means that, although tolerance of the idiosyncracies of others is often seen as a virtue, it must have limits: to a certain extent, intolerance of the self-assertiveness of others should not be discouraged unless excessive, for moderate self-assertiveness is also necessary for the well-being of society. It is thus a matter of keeping the propensities inherent in human nature in a better balance: as we have seen, this is the task of morality.

**Education**
Improving education can have very far-reaching effects on society, not the least being the empowerment of women. This is itself an important factor in population control: in under-developed countries improvement in education has been followed by a decrease in family size.

Here I want to emphasise education's contribution to the society's value system. Many will say that the acquisition of values should take place at the mother's knee, and certainly that is where it starts. Individuals who grow up in homes where they receive sensitive loving care coupled with gentle and appropriate discipline are those most likely to be prosocial with their peers, secure in themselves, and thus able to contribute to building more egalitarian societies (e.g., Cassidy & Shaver, 2008).

In fact, our values can be influenced by experience throughout life, and inculcating societal values is one task of education, both formal and informal. Currently, education is inevitably directed largely to teaching people how to succeed in the competition for jobs. Somehow, amongst society's needs, room must be found for education about the nature of personal relationships and, most especially, it must emphasise the values and the goals of parenthood. This is especially important because the nature of society is changing and future parents, especially young men, need help in understanding children's needs and the responsibilities of parenthood. (Of course, human societies can take many forms, but I am considering the form at present prevalent in Europe and the USA.)

In the past, individual needs of parents and social conventions have been allowed to dictate parenting styles, resulting in maladaptive obstetric techniques, a prejudice against breast feeding, the unnecessary use of wet-nurses, the confinement of children to the nursery, and so on. For most of the time, the boot should be on the other foot, with the child's needs dictating societal conventions about the upbringing of children (Hrdy, 1999). Education should include the learning of parenting techniques, and be aimed at raising the status of parenthood and imparting pride in being a parent.

What many see as educational success involves imparting the ability to use modern ways of thinking and modern technologies. Inevitably, in the present world all children pass through an educational system designed to help them to 'succeed': whether they are taught the most important things is an open issue. Children should be encouraged to develop their creativity, the more so since ways of thinking and technologies are changing all the time. But education must also foster a greater consciousness that the goals of an harmonious society must be seen to include everyone's interests, and also the means to achieve them. A better society must be seen not as a pipe dream of academics but as an achievable goal whose realisation is in the interests of every individual. This will require sensitivity, for the goal of an harmonious society must be seen not as dictated by authority, but a desideratum of every individual. Improving education has been shown to have far-reaching effects on many aspects of social life, including the empowerment of women, though there is a danger that democratic politics may lead to political polarisation (Jamieson, 2013). Good parenting and the desire for more egalitarian societies are most likely to be achieved if parents are not burdened by poverty or distracted by riches, in other words if they live in a more egalitarian society of the type we are trying to create (for discussion, see Roemer, 1996).

Issues of tremendous importance include the teaching of a balanced view of beliefs and values that others see as controversial. Even the teaching of political awareness can lead to the polarisation of political views (Jamieson, 2013). The issue of religious schools is of tremendous importance in the UK. It is argued that parents should have the freedom to choose how their children are educated. But if children are taught in school what they should believe, they will inevitably see children educated in other 'faith' schools as misguided, and the seeds of future prejudice or conflict have been sown. A multi-cultural society has been an aim of the UK government, but encouraging single faith schools is surely counter-productive. In the schools in Northern Ireland, where the schools were either Catholic or Protestant, a research worker commented *'it would seem that children in both types of school are being denied the means to understand each other's heritage'* (Murray, 1995).

## Human rights and responsibilities

Most societies recognise certain human rights. These are mostly similar across cultures but differ in some respects. For instance, in many cultures, and until recently in our own, women were denied some rights enjoyed by men. As a slightly different case, many Jews and many Palestinians believe in their right to Palestine.

The supposedly definitive Universal Declaration of Human Rights was issued by the United Nations in 1948. It is unnecessary here to refer to the content of its 30 Articles, as they are almost second nature to most westerners. It has, however, one deficiency that is demonstrated by comparison with its Islamic equivalent.

The Universal Islamic Declaration of Human Rights was issued by the Islamic Council in 1981. The preamble of the Islamic Declaration states that it *'... is based on the Qur'an and the Sunnah and has been compiled by eminent Muslim scholars and representatives of Islamic movements and thought'*. It has frequent references to the Islamic holy books and assumes that morality should be absolute and unchanging. Though broadly similar to the UN document, it has frequent references to Muslim beliefs and differs in a number of particular respects from the UN Statement. This has led to considerable controversy, especially over the rights of women in Islamic countries and the laxity of sexual morality in the West. I do not intend to enter that debate, but one difference between the UN document and the Islamic declaration is highly significant in the present context: the Islamic Declaration emphasises not only the rights of individuals but also their duties. For instance, it mentions the duty to protest against injustice, to defend the rights of others, to protest and strive against oppression, to search after truth, and to respect the religious feelings of others. It also gives the poor entitlement to a share in the wealth of the rich, insists that the community has a duty to look after orphans, and states that all means of production should be utilised in the interests of the community. The African Charter on Human and Peoples' Rights (1981) carries a similar message in its preamble.

The Universal (United Nations) Declaration has virtually no reference to the individual's duties to society. This perhaps reflects the circumstances in which it was compiled, just after the defeat of three authoritarian regimes in World War II. There are only very general references to duties in Article 1 of the UN Declaration (Everyone *'should act towards one another in a spirit of brotherhood'*) and Article 29 (*'Everyone has duties to the community in which alone the free and full development of his personality is possible'*), but the duties are not further defined. The UN Declaration is not, indeed should not be, related to any particular religion or to religion in general, but an obligatory relation between rights and duties is surely essential in any society. Indeed, it is emphasised in many Christian sources (e.g. The Common Good: Catholic Bishops' Conference of England and Wales, undated).

The omission of adequate mention of responsibilities from the UN Declaration is regrettable. Rights cannot exist without responsibilities. For an harmonious society, every citizen should be conscious of the benefits received from the status of a 'citizen', and recognise that they, by enjoying those benefits, carry responsibilities. Reciprocally, of course, society has the duty to ensure that individuals have the opportunity to exercise their rights.

Like moral precepts, 'rights' are usually seen as unchangeable, or 'inalienable' as the American Constitution puts it. This leads to difficulties. The Second Amendment of the United States Constitution (1791) contains these words:

*A well-regulated Militia being necessary to the security of a free State, the right of the people to keep and bear arms shall not be infringed.*

Abundant evidence indicates that the widespread availability of weapons is a major factor in the high rate of homicide in the United States, yet the perceived authority of the Second Amendment is used by interested parties to preserve the present situation. This continued reverence for the Second Amendment illustrates the dangers in a failure to recognise that times change. In this case financial considerations are involved, and the 'gun lobby' has considerable political leverage.

Other problems arise with the so-called 'Right to Personal Autonomy' which is properly justified in some contexts as a means for protecting individuals from others of higher status, but is an inevitable source of conflict between parent and the maturing child. In western cultures, a degree of autonomy is necessary for the individual's sense of being a unique person and a free agent (Nucci & Lee, 1992), yet it may conflict with the duties inherent in personal relationships, with group loyalties and duties to society (Hinde, 2002).

External threats can lead to bending the rules. The Geneva Conventions for prisoners of war laid down strict rules on prisoners' rights and how they should be treated. However, the destruction of the Twin Towers on September 11$^{th}$ 2001 led to the use of the US Guantanamo detention camp for suspected terrorists, some of whom were kept for years without trial (Sands, 2008). The use of the most devastating forms of torture for extracting information was said to be justified by the belief that further attacks on the USA could be prevented by obtaining statements in this way. Freedom of speech, opinion, and movement have come to be seen as essential, but it is not always recognised that it becomes logically necessary to grant the same rights to others. In the UK, recently, steps taken to enhance 'national security' after the terrorist attacks in London have come into conflict with the right to personal autonomy.

This conflict between the need for moral rules and human rights to be absolute and yet, at the same time, to have some flexibility has no general solution. In the end, it would seem, any deviation from the rules must be entrusted to the wisdom of a body whose judgements are generally accepted as authoritative. Such a body is not always easy to find, but a precedent exists in the International Court of Justice. For instance, the Court has ruled against the threat or use of nuclear weapons except in self-defence when the survival of the state is at stake: on their use in self-defence the Court was divided.

**Individualism and collectivism**
These two concepts, while not academically respectable, are useful in discussion of trends in our societies (Triandis, 1991). At present, western societies seem to be steered by selfish assertiveness, self-interest and greed, in other words, to be becoming increasingly individualistic. This individualism of western societies involves a focus on the individual, to the neglect of others, the group and society. We see ourselves as distinct non-identical entities. By contrast, members of a collectivist society tend to see others as closely linked to themselves and others. The contrast between the two was brought home to me by two letters, one from a colleague who had been working in Cameroon, who wrote she was *alternately talking to students there and in Berkeley. A Cameroonian forester explained that he saw himself as a bridge between his father and his son, and didn't perceive himself as a free-standing individual at all. Among the Californian undergraduates emphasis on personal individuality is well-known: the contrast was quite disorienting* (T. Rowell, personal communication). The second letter came from a UK colleague with Quaker sympathies who, as a governor of a primary school, had been puzzled by a school inspector's report that 'spirituality education' needed improvement. His reflections on how to teach spirituality led him to *'my grandmother-me-granddaughter' model. I am fortunate in having known all four of my grandparents, and in having good relations with seven grandchildren. One grandmother, for example, of good Methodist stock, was one whom I greatly valued, and so influenced me. Similarly, I hope that any particular grandchild will take away something of interest from me, and hence in some way from grandmother. By extrapolation, this brings in a whole set of influences (in a way surely that is indeed special to the human animal) – one of which includes Jesus (as interpreted by his all-too-fallible recorders). Which is why some people would rate me as a Christian. However, another strand of my 'spiritual' background comes from those good friends who happen to be Muslim or Jewish, or whatever. So, perhaps I am a Muslim also* (K. Hill, personal communication).

On another issue, mentioned already, the Christian rationale for 'good' behaviour is sometimes seen as lying in its consequences for the individual rather than the group. In parts of the Sermon on the Mount good behaviour is recommended because it leads to good outcomes for the individual: 'Blessed are the merciful, for they shall obtain mercy' (Matthew, 5, 7). Generalising, one can say that the balance between regard for consequences on the actor and consequences on others or on the group is loaded in favour of the actor in the West today. A new morality should have greater regard for others and for the community than we have at present.

I should emphasize that I am not saying that Christianity as practised has no regard for others, or that it is a predominantly selfish religion: on the contrary, it abounds with admonitions to help others, to be charitable and so on. The point being made is that too often behaviour is motivated by personal profit or salvation, not the communal good. Some reformers in the Islamic world see Islam as in danger of being contaminated by western individualism and the associated western decadence.

The idea that a society could be composed entirely of individuals interested solely in their own welfare and happiness is a contradiction in terms: it simply could not exist. Nor, for different reasons, could a society composed entirely of entirely unselfish, cooperative individuals: it would fall prey to outside forces and, anyway, people are just not like that and never will be. It is evident that so far we have failed to find an adequate compromise. Can we do better? Efforts are being made to build 'Intentional Communities' (*www.ic.org* and *www.cohousing.org*). I have no personal experience of this way of living, but they seem to incorporate many of the values discussed in the previous pages. '*Cohousing provides the privacy we are accustomed to within the community we seek.*'

In fact, we do not have to look far for evidence that we can give as heavy a weighting to the well-being of others as to ourselves. The nature of love and of intimate personal relationships provides ample illustrations of unselfish interpersonal attitudes and behaviour.

Evidence is accruing that, even amongst western societies, those containing many sub-groups tend to have fewer internal tensions and more trust than those of a similar size whose members seldom meet socially. Such groups can, by increasing interpersonal understanding, reduce tensions in the society as a whole. We need to invigorate the smaller groups within our society, thereby enhancing our 'social capital' (Putnam, 2000; Szreter, 2005). Unfortunately, in the USA, and probably elsewhere, the small scale societies and groups that provided experience for all their members in voting and direct decision-making, like churches and community groups, have been declining for over 30 years. We need especially 'bridging social capital' that fosters links between such intra-societal groupings.

**Summary**
Many of today's problems are consequences of the ever-increasing world population: the need to curb population growth is insufficiently recognised. Modern living requires that we should be able to form constructive relationships, and achieve real understanding and empathy with our peers. This could be facilitated by adjustments to our educational system, and especially education for parenthood. The privilege of living in a society in which human rights are recognised implies also responsibilities to our peers and to that society. Reciprocally, society must provide the conditions in which individuals can exercise their rights. At present, western societies are structured largely with the success of individuals in mind. Our social structures and world-view need to be shifted so that the good of the collective is seen as a goal of individuals.

# Part V
# Adjustments Are Possible

In previous chapters I have argued that we live in a society that is less satisfactory than it should or could be. I have tried to pinpoint some of the problems and I suggest that many of the difficulties stem from the institutions we have created in the partly mistaken belief that they would be in our own interests. I believe the solution must lie in a change of heart, a change in the way we see the world. Many will say that one cannot change the world. The next chapter argues that we already have the tools to do so.

Chapter 10

# We Have the Potential

**Introduction**
Early in our evolutionary history, natural and cultural selection operated to promote individual success in competition with in-group peers as well as to cooperate with them to promote the success of one's own group in competition with other groups. It is inevitable that these two propensities should often be in conflict. That does not mean we are always conscious of conflict, in part because our conscience usually keeps us on the right track. In the course of group-living we have acquired the potential to develop a world-view involving values conducive to equitable societies. In spite of that, a high proportion of individuals have inadequate food, water and shelter or lack facilities for education, medical care, and other amenities that could reasonably be expected in a modern society. At the same time a considerable proportion of our population have far more than they need. To cite one more example, the ten most expensive boroughs in London are said to have a combined property value equal to that of Wales, Scotland and Northern Ireland combined (Editorial, *The Observer*, 03/02/13).

Many of our present problems indicate that we have not got the balance between prosociality and selfish assertiveness quite right. Neither extreme would be viable: what we have at present is tipped towards self-interest with too little emphasis on the well-being of others. I put the onus for this in large part on some of the institutions we have fostered in good faith for our general benefit, most especially the competitiveness resulting by extension from what is seen as appropriate in the marketplace. Competitiveness has spread throughout society and, if excessive, can poison even recreational activities. Since the decisions we make are influenced by the culture in which we live, we need a small shift in how individuals see the world. The possibility of a degree of lability in the moral system is in harmony with the nature of morality as a system, evolved through dialectical influences between what people do and what is seen as acceptable in the society, and capable of adjustment. However, change will always be constrained: it will involve a development of what has gone before, and it will be limited by human propensities.

Because moral principles and practices must be *seen as* absolute, although with some lability, and because change affects some aspects of society but not others, we must accept that some moral issues from the past are losing their relevance (e.g., premarital cohabitation), while other examples from the past or other cultures have ongoing importance (e.g., the need to inhibit excessive self-assertiveness. In this chapter I argue that many of the propensities we need are present in our nature already and need only to be brought to the surface.

We have seen that the propensity to develop in a certain way may remain dormant for many generations if the external conditions appropriate for its development are absent. This chapter cites some aspects of behaviour that, though conducive to group well-being, are absent or reduced in western cultures, but present in some degree elsewhere. They provide ample evidence that cultural change towards a more desirable society is possible and achievable.

**Cultural differences**

We have already seen some examples of the relations between cultural norms and the behaviour of individuals in test situations. An important edited volume (Chen & Rubin, 2011) provides numerous examples of how cultural differences in child-rearing practices are related to societal differences in prosocial and selfishly assertive behaviour. To take some examples that illustrate the present thesis, children's cooperative behaviour declines with increasing urbanisation (Graves & Graves, 1983), and children living in extended families in which they are required to assume family responsibilities tend to show more prosocial and cooperative behaviour than those in economically complex, class-structured societies (Eisenberg & Fabes, 1998). Children in East Asian and some South American countries are more cooperative in their social interactions than North American children (Farver, Kim & Lee, 1995). Such differences in prosocial behaviour are related to differences in cultural beliefs and norms (Chen, 2011; Stevenson-Hinde, 2011). That immigrants can adjust to new cultures, if not immediately at least in a generation or two, shows that possibilities for change exist in every society. Indeed, if there are differences between cultures, this in itself means that some change is possible (Edwards, 2000).

Prosociality in children in Western (and probably all other) societies is enhanced if the caregiver is sensitively responsive to the child's needs and uses gentle and reasoned discipline (reviewed in Cassidy & Shaver, 2008). The child's social relationships in later years can also have profound effects: growing up in a highly competitive or militaristic environment may, but need not, swing the balance between selfish assertiveness and prosociality in favour of the former. Less dramatic changes in either direction consequential on the dialectical relations between what people do and what they are supposed to do were mentioned in earlier chapters.

Thus the growing cross-cultural literature, together with that on child development, shows that a propensity to feel concern for the well-being of others can be encouraged by sensitive rearing practices. Although early childhood experiences may be seen as laying a foundation for prosocial behaviour, change is possible beyond childhood, and indeed throughout life. St. Paul's conversion on the road to Damascus may or may not be a myth, but more recent comparable cases have been documented. For example, Colby and Damon (1995) cite the case of a girl brought up in Alabama with strong racial prejudices. Forced against her will in college to sit at a table with a black girl, she came to like and respect the black girl and eventually dedicated most of her life to working for civil rights.

**Concepts of fairness**
We have seen that 'Exchange theories' (pp. 38-40) provide powerful insights into the nature of interpersonal relationships. Important to this approach is that exchange should be seen by the participants as 'fair'. The important words here are 'seen to be' – fairness is a subjective concept. Now societal culture both influences and is influenced by how the individuals behave to each other (Figure 1). Of particular interest here are the results of the 'Dictator game' and 'Ultimatum game' as played in different societies. In both these games, one player (the proposer) is given a sum of money and told to share it with another (the recipient). In the Dictator game, once the offer has been made, the game is over. With students in industrial societies most proposers take the self-interested course and offer nothing, but a few offer around 50%. Apparently some proposers prefer to avoid marked unfairness.

In the Ultimatum game, the recipient can accept or refuse the offer: if he accepts, both keep what they have got, but if he rejects the offer neither gets anything. Here, in industrial societies, proposers offer around 50% and recipients reject offers of less than 20%. It might seem sensible for the recipient to accept whatever was offered, however little, but apparently they often felt low offers were unfair and rejected them. These results again suggest that participants try to gain as much as they can, but also have a sense of fairness and reject low offers as though such offers were insulting (Hauser, 2006).

But can these results, mostly obtained with student subjects, be generalised? When the ultimatum game was played in small-scale societies, the results were rather different, and related to the cultural norms in the society in question. For instance, a group of horticulturists in Peru whose cultural practices involve little cooperation or sharing outside the family, made very low offers (15%) and rarely rejected low offers. By contrast, the Aché of Paraguay, where hunters share what they kill with other families in the group, typically offer more than 40% and accept low offers (Henrich, Boyd, et al., 2005; see also Gurven & Winking, 2008)).

There are many variants of these games, of particular interest being those in which the games are repeated with the same individuals, and only a small part of this work has been abstracted here. Furthermore, it must be said that there are many difficulties in conducting such games in diverse cultures. Nevertheless the data appear to be entirely compatible with the view that humans have a propensity to seek for fairness that may partially counter self-interest, but that what is considered fair varies with the culture.

This point is compatible with the scheme illustrated in Fig. 1. The culture (almost by definition) permeates the whole society, and to achieve our goal of a proper balance between benefits to the self and benefits to the community, we must make a slight change in our cultural values.

### 'Egalitarian' societies

We have seen that many of the ills in our societies are related to the marked differences in wealth and influence between those at the top and those at the bottom of our hierarchical worlds (pp. 78-80). It is improbable, and perhaps undesirable, that such differences in wealth could be totally eliminated, but it is clearly desirable that they should be drastically reduced.

Strong evidence that humans can avoid marked discrepancies in influence and possessions between individuals comes from studies of nomadic hunter/gatherer societies. We have seen that Boehm, on the basis of extensive field-work and a survey of the anthropological literature, has shown that at least the great majority of surviving hunter/gatherers live in groups with several adult males, amongst whom relationships are egalitarian. This does not mean that life in such groups is all sweetness and light, nor that the individuals in these groups lack self assertiveness, but rather that, in discussions amongst males, any individual who is seen to be becoming too big for his boots is taken down a peg by other group members. A selfishly assertive propensity to dominate is still present, but any individual who allows it to become overt is suppressed. Even displays of anger may be frowned upon, and if one individual belittles, bullies or otherwise attempts to control another, others support the victim.

This ethos of support for any individual male being put upon by another is interpreted by Boehm as indicating an egalitarian ideal. It can perhaps be seen as resulting from a fear that the bully, if not restrained, may infringe the autonomy of others including any who support the victim, and implies that the supporters can rely on a group with an egalitarian orientation. We have seen that some authorities prefer an interpretation in terms of Machiavellian self-seeking (Whiten, 1994; Erdal & Whiten, 1996). In either case we can readily empathise with such behaviour: one feels irritated (to say the least) with colleagues who talk too much or try to lead a group or group discussion when it is not appropriate for them to do so ('loud mouths'). Such behaviour is entirely in keeping with the moralistic aggression directed against those who behave too assertively in hunter/gatherer societies. It is also in keeping with the view that what mattered in the evolution of prosocial behaviour to other group members is that *other people* should behave prosocially. However, in most western societies, moralistic aggression is inhibited because those who show it might fear being seen as too self-important, self-righteous or self-assertive. Again, have we got the balance right?

The processes used to suppress overly self-assertive individuals in hunter/gatherer groups may originate from gossip spreading the view that the offender is being too self-important. The signs of social disapproval may be quite subtle, but the offenders are usually sensitive to them. If subtle signs are inadequate, they may lead to the offender receiving cool treatment from others, a refusal to follow his suggestions, ridicule, and social isolation. In rare cases it may lead to the execution of the offender: in such cases, apparently to avoid the dangers of escalation, it may be arranged that the executioner should be a relative. But such extreme cases are rare, apparently because the desirability of a social ethos of near-egalitarianism is generally recognised. Individuals take care not to be seen as self-important: for instance, the successful hunter will downplay the value of the animal he has killed and display exaggerated modesty about his achievement. What is important is that each group member should respect the individual autonomy of others. The basic issue is not the absence of a leader, but the ethos of the essential equality of all, and the willingness to act assertively to maintain that ethos. Individuals must be careful when moving from a family head role, where dominance is permitted and even required, to the role of a band member amongst band members, where the egalitarian ethos must be respected. Tension is not entirely absent, but is apparently preferred to that arising from inequalities.

Although within a household dominance of one individual by another is usual, these hunter/gatherers are characterised not only by an overall egalitarian ethos among the (mostly male) heads of families but also by an ethic of sharing between households. This involves primarily the sharing of meat after a large animal has been killed: a successful hunter may enjoy extra respect and other rewards for his success, but is expected to share at least some of the meat with others and be very reticent about his achievement (Kaplan & Hill, 1985). Since a high proportion of attempts to kill large animals are unsuccessful, and luck as well as differences in skill plays a certain role in this, sharing meat helps to ensure that everyone gets an adequate supply. Small food items are usually not shared.

While it is recognised that some individuals have special skills, this is not seen as permitting them to dominate others or to have a special status in the group. Such an individual may be allowed to lead in an appropriate context, but he will be watched closely for signs of bossiness. The suppression of overtly assertive behaviour is conspicuous in the decision-making of the group when important decisions are made by consensus amongst the household heads. Leaders with special expertise are allowed to be only 'first among equals'. Usually they are required to be generous and to have other positive qualities, and they must behave with care in case they are seen to be breaching the ethos of equality.

A more recent example is provided by the population of St. Kilda, a remote, largely barren island off the north-west coast of Scotland, inhabited until 1930. The islanders lived mainly on birds and fish, as there were only small areas that could be cultivated. A steward made yearly visits to the island to collect rents demanded by the landlord, the MacLeods of Dunvegan (Isle of Skye, Scotland). The small areas of arable land were divided into hundreds of strips which were parcelled out amongst the islanders by their Parliament for three year periods and then redistributed. There was an intricate web of ownership rights, always subject to the overweening rights of the kin group and the community. The cliffs, where birds were taken in hazardous climbs, also varied greatly in productivity and were re-distributed every year, each family harvesting its own ledges (Martin, 1698).

I am not suggesting for one moment that we should abandon our way of life and try to imitate that of hunter-gatherers. Although, like them, we are still members of *Homo sapiens*, we are not hunter-gatherers. But we can abstract generalisations from the way they live and use them to nudge our way of living towards something more equitable than we have at the moment. As stressed above, 'egalitarianism' is a misleading term. Just because people differ, there will always be some who see the way ahead better than others. A major job of democracy is to see that their goals are generally acceptable goals, and that they do not exceed their briefs.

**Some features of our own culture**
Some will say that that is all very well, but it does not mean that a greater degree of egalitarianism could flourish in the complexity of modern societies. Certainly it would require major changes in people's values and world-view. But the persistence of these more egalitarian societies into the modern world provides an opportunity for us to see just how they worked from the position of outside observers. Of course, we must be aware that they do not give us a full picture of how people felt: anthropological studies tell us little about how individuals deal with their own desires to be leaders.

At the risk of repetition, it is appropriate to stress that the values and propensities important in these egalitarian societies are potentially present in ourselves. In the first place, we live in groups, we enjoy group life, and we possess the complex cognitive abilities necessary for handling the several relationships that each of us is engaged in. Second, familiarity breeds trust of other group members, including the capacity to cooperate with one or more others to achieve a goal. This, apparently, is something that even chimpanzees often seem to lack. Third, we all have a propensity to want to control others (Bandura, 1997), but usually recognise that in most situations it is not appropriate. Fourth, at the same time we do not like to be bossed by others. We have a propensity to take down anyone who threatens the autonomy of others. Thus most people enjoy group life, and abhor excessive self-importance in others. Most people value their own autonomy but recognise that this requires respect for that of others. This requires a norm of equality: although we find it difficult to define what we mean by equality and how to achieve it, we still want to put down those members of our own group who think too much of themselves. Fifth, although people do not like to admit it, we all value the good opinions of others. Sixth, we would like to live in a society in which relationships could have much less tension than is often the case today, a society in which we maintained our own autonomy and were not bossed by others. Seventh, although we like our own autonomy, we are willing to share (Botsman & Rogers, 2011).

Two features of modern life need special mention. For the disapproval of peers to be effective, individuals must know what others are doing. Most people have an intense interest in other people's affairs, though few will own up to it (Dunbar, 1996). Gossip is seen by many as the province of busy bodies or of people who have nothing better to do, but in practice it can be an important channel of communication, informing people what others are up to. So perhaps the negative evaluation that gossip is given is a little too harsh.

People often deny enjoying having a gossip. Interestingly, it seems to concern the bad things that other people do rather than the good. We have already noticed how the media tend to report murders, rapes and robberies more than the prosocial things that people do. This bias towards an interest in the bad could play a part in limiting our self-assertiveness by increasing the sensitivity of others to notice any tendency to anti-social behaviour.

An extreme issue concerns the status of the 'whistle-blower'. If an employee thinks that the work he is being asked to carry out is either illegal or immoral, he can publicise his misgivings, thereby perhaps breaking an undertaking that he took (or was forced to take) as a condition of his employment and risking the employer's response, including losing his job and all the consequences that would entail for his family, and even prosecution. Or he can remain silent and carry the guilt of participating in an improper enterprise. The punishment for whistle-blowing can be extremely severe. Mordechai Vanunu is perhaps an extreme example. As an Israeli technician, employed in the Dimona plant, he found that he was engaged in a clandestine project to produce plutonium for nuclear weapons. At that time it was not known outside Israel that the country was producing nuclear weapons contrary to international agreements. Vanunu publicised the issue, resigned his post, and fled abroad. He was kidnapped by Israeli police acting under cover and sentenced to 18 years in prison, mostly in solitary confinement. Even when he had served this unjust sentence the Israeli authorities placed severe restrictions on his movements.

So the psychological propensities necessary for a more egalitarian or sharing society are present in virtually everyone. The values held in the egalitarian societies just discussed differ in degree from the values held in much of the modern industrialised world, where selfish assertiveness is encouraged and often seems to predominate. But not everywhere. Japan is an example of a modern society that seems to have moved in an egalitarian direction not incompatible with those just described. Many of its characteristics are shared by other East Asian cultures.

**The example of Japan**
Amongst modern societies, Japan deserves attention because its culture has come to resemble that with which we are familiar yet differs in some relevant and important characteristics bearing on the theme of this book (Macfarlane, 2008). Japanese and other Asian ways of thinking are very different from those of western societies in many ways, some quite fundamental. For instance, in conflicts between formal and intuitive reasoning, European Americans tend to rely on the former rather than the latter, while Chinese and Koreans rely more on intuitive strategies (Norenzayan et al., 2002). This difference is likely to apply to all East Asian countries and underlies differences in philosophies, religion and basic ways of thinking. Japanese society is also very different from the sort of society that many of us would like in that, for instance, it is very hierarchical. But there are two characteristics that are of interest in the present context, the nature of everyday interactions, and the capacity for sharing.

Japan's society seems almost incomprehensible to outsiders. In Japan, sometimes described as a village transported to a city, harmony is an apparent goal of almost all interpersonal behaviour. To the foreigner, interactions and public relationships seem deferential, even defensive and obsequious: people warily avoid any sign of pushiness or aggression, but seem as though trying to ingratiate themselves with each other. *'Tentative harmony, trust, relationality, and desire to please and be pleased, all these are stressed purposes of greeting etiquette'. 'Politeness and etiquette come before morals and before law'*, and it seems more important to be polite than to tell the truth. In Japan *'Affection is more important than logic or ethics'* (Macfarlane, 2008).

In Japan there is no judging God, nor any polytheistic system of powerful gods who must be placated. Language is used largely to avoid confrontation, and argument and debate are avoided. In the past the Japanese desire for harmony even extended to the building, after a battle, of two kinds of shrine, one for the winners of the battle and one for the losers: this was believed to calm down the losers' anger and soothe the negative side of the past. The need to maintain a harmonious atmosphere is deeply ingrained in the Japanese psyche, and the need to put down anyone who is becoming selfishly assertive is described as the *'need to hit the nail flush with the wood'*. Even in childhood the fear of being seen as pushy is reinforced both by positive reward and by punishment (or threat of punishment) so that it is incorporated into the self-concept of an individual.

This differs only in degree from our own behaviour when we disguise our feelings about our friends or friends' friends for fear of offending them. We follow the rules of politeness not because we fear God's punishment, but ultimately because we fear the disapproval or ridicule of our friends. We are uncomfortable when someone else appears to be acting out of turn or being too self-assertive, but often refrain from comment for fear of being impolite or causing unpleasantness.

It is difficult to assess the situation from newspaper reports, but New Orleans, Haiti and the Philippines have all suffered major disasters in recent years, and in each case it seems that the disaster was followed by extensive looting. This was not the case in Japan after the triple disasters of earthquake, tsunami and damage to a nuclear power station: little looting occurred, and the people, though desperate for food, still waited in line for groceries. In some of the devastated areas the survivors banded together and began to divide the tasks necessary for their future joint survival – boiling water, scavenging for food and petrol, preparing food. Within at least some areas they established communities, with an impromptu governing body and communication with neighbouring refugee centres. The stoicism and self-sacrifice, the quiet bravery in the face of tragedy, were remarkable to western reporters. Even the organised crime syndicates kept an eye out for looters and provided extensive humanitarian aid, though later they sought to profit from clearing up the mess.

These differences are based on impressionistic accounts and may be overstated, but they seem real. No doubt the difference from New Orleans, Haiti and the Philippines has many causes, including Japan's long history, its isolation, and its tradition of surmounting natural disasters. Those affected in New Orleans and Haiti were mostly the very poor whose lives had previously been a struggle for survival, allowing little space for feelings about their own community. It is perhaps as a consequence of such differences that the honest and altruistic behaviour of many Japanese after the disaster seems to have been part of the Japanese psyche.

In support of that view, a concept of corporate social responsibility was central in the feudal period in certain areas of Japan, for instance the Ohmi district, not far from Kyoto. The merchants there subscribed to the 'Sanpo Yoshi' policy (three ways policy) which stated that for a business to be successful its activities must be 'good for the seller, good for the buyer, and good for the society'. It was held that 'greed' and pure profit motives were the source of many evils, and only by following the Sanpo Yoshi would a merchant be fully successful. The merchants from this area were well known for travelling all over Japan, returning to their own towns during planting and harvest times, when they shared with their peers what they had learnt about the markets elsewhere (L. Shimizu, personal communication).

However one must be careful of generalisations. The sense of community is always influenced by the environment: some observers pointed out that the response to the tsunami disaster might have been very different amongst a younger, predominantly entrepreneurial city population where western influences have weakened the traditional importance of social integration. And there are other factors operating to maintain prosociality in Japan. There are rewards for turning in lost property to the police station, and also penalties for failure to turn in property that you have found. There is a strong police presence. Nevertheless, in terms of the model I have been using, it seems as though the balance between the propensities for prosociality and selfish assertiveness are traditionally maintained more in favour of prosociality than is usual in the West, and this seems to be due to the value of social cohesion being embedded in the self-system early in life, aided by fear of social punishment.

In Japan prosocial behaviour is accentuated and usually appears to westerners to be predominant. But the propensity for selfish assertiveness is still present and responsive to circumstances. Individuals must avoid arousing it in others.

**Changes in values in modern societies**
Although we feel that the moral precepts that guide our behaviour are immutable, some change is occurring all the time. I have already referred to the changes in the acceptability of divorce. Comparable dialectical processes have led to changes in many of the values

surrounding sexual behaviour. Thus, before World War II in my university, if a male student were found to have a woman in his room after a certain hour, he was almost inevitably expelled. Since that time the situation has changed, and students' personal relationships are normally considered as their own affair (Dormor, 2004). Sharing is another human propensity that is suppressed by the possessiveness that accompanies selfish assertiveness, though the absurdity of every household possessing a power drill is all too obvious (Botsman & Rogers, 2011).

Three cases of changes in morality in relatively recent times have been carefully analysed by Appiah (2010): duelling and the slave trade, which disappeared in the mid-nineteenth century, and foot-binding amongst the élite in China which endured until the turn of the $19^{th}/20^{th}$ centuries. In each case the moral issues were known, though perhaps not properly digested, beforehand, but the demise of the practice occurred only when there was a change in values. Appiah describes this as a change in honour. Honour, in Appiah's view, is a matter of the respect one receives, or can expect to receive, from others in one's own social category. Honour can be distinct from morality: for instance, challenging another gentleman to a duel could be seen as the honourable thing to do and at the same time as morally wrong.

Duelling was illegal in the UK but the authorities turned a blind eye on it so long as it involved only members of the upper classes. Amongst the latter it was a matter of honour to issue a challenge if you were insulted by another 'gentleman', and a matter of honour to respond if you received one. When duelling was taken up by members of the middle classes, businessmen and such like, it ceased to be an 'honourable gentleman's' prerogative, and came to be seen as ridiculous. In this change, newspaper comments and cartoons played an important role.

Foot-binding amongst the Chinese élite involved the deformation of the feet of girls and women by tight binding over a long period. It was extremely painful for the woman, but was tolerated because a woman's bound foot was seen as exquisitely beautiful. The practice was limited to the élite, and may have owed its popularity to the fact that a woman with bound feet could walk only with difficulty and would therefore find it difficult to stray. The end of foot-binding was largely a consequence of the increasing influence of foreigners. European merchants arrived in the ports, and missionaries penetrated inland, bringing not only Christianity but also modernity. The natural feet of the foreign women brought into relief the absurdity of the distorted feet of those whose feet had been bound. The Chinese élite came to recognise that the practice was seen as ridiculous by the foreigners and brought the country into disrepute. National reputation was as important as women's welfare in bringing about the change.

Slavery in the British Empire had been in the country's economic interests and the ending of the slave trade and of slavery in the British Empire may have been facilitated somewhat by a decrease in the profitability of West Indian sugar. However, the change occurred in spite of sugar's abiding economic value to the country: conflicting views of the factors involved in the suppression of slavery have been discussed by Drescher (2010). Appiah's interesting analysis puts the emphasis on the role of reformers, Quakers and others, in convincing the country that a practice that was so immoral should not be allowed. This led to petitions to the UK Parliament with hundreds of thousands of signatures. The working classes came to identify with the slaves and the position of servility and the unremitting labour that they had to endure. In this case the standards of honour and morality were identical: slave owners lost honour in the sight of their peers.

The common factor in these three cases is that a practice previously seen as acceptable and honourable in the relevant section of society came to be seen as wrong. With duelling and foot-binding the change occurred in the section of society in which the practice was endemic, though the change was influenced by the opinions of a wider public. With the slave trade it was a much wider public that helped to bring about the change. How far this can be generalised to other changes in morality is open to question: changes in the law about homosexuality in Britain were due to relatively few members of the intellectual élite, and initially the changes remained unacceptable to many and perhaps to the majority of the population.

In each case the change can be seen as exemplifying the dialectic between what people do and what they are supposed to do, as suggested in chapter 2. And in each case the change in opinion can be seen as a change in the self-concepts and world-views of those involved under the influence of outside opinion. The important point for the present discussion is that they show that change can be made to happen.

**Inducing change in world-views**
The important question, of course, is how can changes in world-view be brought about in modern societies? I must emphasise again that I am

not trying to promote a major change in societies next year, but rather to call attention to the need for some adjustment in the ways in which we see the world. Change will certainly be difficult and slow to achieve, but if we delay, things may get worse.

An example is provided by the work of the non-governmental organisation 'Integrity Action'. Much, but by no means all, of its work involves rectifying low or mid-level corruption in aid given to developing countries. Across the board, over 80% of the aid given for infrastructure projects and 30% of that given for public services is lost through corruption. Schools, hospitals and roads are not built or are built to inadequate standards, and the community is denied the possibility of advancement.

Tackling corruption is inherently difficult because its multifaceted nature demands diverse responses. The aim of Integrity Action is to build a culture of integrity by supporting citizens and organisations to develop systems that promote integrity. That involves not only working with the community leaders but also with the citizens themselves – from the top down and from the bottom up: *http://www.integrityaction.org /what-integrity.*

Given evidence of corruption, Integrity Action does not seek immediately to blow the whistle, but uses the evidence to influence public officials and other stakeholders (including those affected by the malpractice) to improve the situation. Because corruption is inherently complex, and because instances of corruption are diverse, it is impossible to represent the scope of its work in a few words but, as an example, a company was given a grant to supply concrete to enable a new road in Afghanistan to be surfaced to a certain depth. After the company claimed it had done its work the road was found to be surfaced only to a much smaller depth. It seemed that the money for the rest of the concrete had 'disappeared'. Instead of raising public protest, monitors appointed by Integrity Action appealed to the stakeholders affected by the shortfall. They reasoned with the contractors, who were then shamed into rectifying the situation.

Integrity Action's approach is not the only route through which efforts are being made to counter corruption and to alert citizens to the importance of integrity in transactions. I have chosen it because it does not rely solely on narrative reports to assess their success but uses a metric, the 'fix rate'. This is the percentage of identified problems that are resolved to the satisfaction of the stakeholders. This varies widely between countries and with the nature of the problem, but may be higher than ninety per cent.

Integrity Action devotes a proportion of its effort to education. It fosters the ability of citizens to expose failures in the delivery of social services and fosters their ability to participate in local political processes. It is also attempting to introduce an integrity course into law schools, thereby preparing law students to improve the access of disadvantaged groups to justice. More importantly, perhaps, it seeks to disseminate news of is successes so that the value of living in communities with others of integrity becomes more generally appreciated (*http://www.integrityaction.org/integrity-education-network-O*).

**Summary**

In our present society the balance between self-interest and the well-being of the group has drifted towards the former. We need to readjust that balance. That cultures differ indicates that our culture, including our moral values, are not set in stone. Some features of our own behaviour show that we have the propensities necessary for a more equitable society. Some examples of changes in values are cited.

Chapter 11

# Conclusion

In conclusion, it might be helpful to set out the main points of the argument.

Our societies do not function as they should. Both within countries and across countries resources are unfairly distributed. Some will argue that 'fairness' is a tricky concept and there are different ways of assessing what is 'fair'. Many will say that a competitive market economy is best for most people and inevitably results in an uneven distribution of resources. But the data show that many social ills are related to this uneven distribution of resources.

We tend to think that things will improve if we control the activities of those responsible for the distribution of resources. We pass new laws that will constrain the activities of financiers or we seek to improve our political or banking systems. Such changes may help but, with things as they are, there will always be individuals who find their way round the regulations. We cannot put all the blame on politicians or financiers because we are all responsible in some degree. The bottom line is that we are too GREEDY. Not everybody, but most people in some degree. We tend to see the world as lacking morality, and accordingly behave without adequate concern for others.

As an heuristic device I have assumed that we have two propensities: to behave prosocially to others, especially to members of our own group, and with selfish assertiveness. Maintaining a proper balance between these two propensities within one's own group is the function of morality.

In our society, influences flow from the more complex entities to the relatively simple, *and* vice-versa. For example, the values of each subgroup in the society are influenced by the characteristics of its members, and reciprocally the values of the individuals are influenced by those of the group (Figure 1). Thus, how each of us behaves, how we see the world and what we value, matter.

Moral values must be seen as immutable, yet as retaining a limited flexibility in order to cope with changes in society and its increasing complexity. Our distinction between good and bad cannot easily be encapsulated in a few principles or precepts but, in general, actions intended to improve the well-being of our fellows are good, those that improve our own well-being but not that of others are bad – but that is only a starting point for distinguishing good from evil.

To build societies with less tension, we must nudge our world-view and our values away from today's excessive materialism and self-interest, give more precedence to the well-being of others, and focus on values rather than rigid precepts. Change will be slow, but we must never despair.

Morality is often seen as part of religion. I suggest that this is a mistake. Religions have indeed purveyed morality, but religious beliefs have had different origins and goals from those of morality, and do not form a suitable basis for morality. The apparently close relation between religion and morality could have arisen because priests and other religious specialists saw that moral rules would command more respect and be more effective if seen to represent the will of an all-powerful deity.

Given human nature, it is inevitable that many of our decisions should be between incompatible goals. We are seldom faced with simple alternatives between prosociality and selfish assertiveness. One source of our difficulties lies in the institutions we have created for our own purposes. Humans have devised institutions for specific purposes within society. Each institution may contain many roles, and the incumbents of these roles must behave in specified ways, sometimes contrary to accepted morality. Of special importance here is the marketplace. Dealing requires buyers and sellers to distort the truth and encourages greed. Its values spill over into the everyday life of individuals. There is a tendency for the distortion of values in the marketplace to spread into the rest of our lives as winning becomes an over-riding goal.

Many other institutions require individuals to behave in ways at odds with socially accepted values. Our democratic political systems encourage politicians to distort the truth, with an eye on the next election. War is an institution with many roles, each with specified rights and duties: in war, killing can become a duty.

We need an educational system that embraces the nature of personal relationships, especially those between men and women and between parents and children. We must move towards a situation in which moral guidelines are seen not as something outside ourselves, constraining our actions, but as part of ourselves. The route to be taken is being mapped out, albeit slowly, by developmental psychologists and other social scientists.

It will take time, and carrots and sticks may always be necessary, but will be more effective if they do not depend on forces outside our society, like Heaven and Hell. Rather, if used sensitively, the moral indignation of our peers at our misdeeds and their approval of any good deeds, backed up by a legal system, will suffice.

Many of the psychological propensities that would help us to achieve a more equitable society are in our nature, but are suppressed by the need to meet present conventions. The changes we need lie not just in the morality of individuals, and not just in the morality of our leaders. Rather we need a change in the values that pervade society so that more emphasis is placed on the consequences of our actions for others.

# References

Adams, H. (1876). Essays on Anglo-Saxon Law. Boston MA: Little Brown.
Ainsworth, M.D.S., Blehar, M.C., Waters, E. & Wall, S. (1978). Patterns of Attachment. Hillsdale NJ: Erlbaum.
Alexander, R.D. (1979). Darwinism and Human Affairs. Seattle: University of Washington Press.
Appiah, K.A. (2010). The Honor Code. New York: Norton.
Aron, A. & Aron, E.A. (1996). Self and self-expansion in relationships. In Fletcher & Fitness (eds.) Knowledge Structures in Close Relationships, pp. 325-344. Hillsdale NJ: Erlbaum..
Asma, S.T. (2013). Against Fairness. Chicago: University of Chicago Press.
Atran, S. (2010). Talking to The Enemy. London: Allen Lane (Penguin).

Backman, C.W. (1988). The Self: A dialectical approach. Advances in Experimental Psychology, 21, 229-260.
Bandura, A. (1997). Self-Efficacy: The Exercise of Control. New York: Freeman.
Baron-Cohen, S. (1997). The Maladaptive Mind. Hove: Psychology Press
Bateson, M., Nettle, D. & Roberts, G. (2006). Cues of being watched enhance cooperation in a real world setting. Biological Letters (Royal Society), 2, 412-4.
Bateson, P. (1989). Does evolutionary biology contribute to ethics? Biology and Philosophy, 4, 287-301.
Bateson, P. & Gluckman, P. (2011). Plasticity, Robustness, Development & Evolution. Cambridge: Cambridge University Press.
Benedict, R. (1934). Patterns of Culture. Boston MA: Houghton Mifflin.
Bishops Conference of England and Wales. (2010). Choosing the Common Good. London: Alive Publishing.
Boehm, C. (1991). Hierarchy in the Forest. Cambridge MA: Harvard University Press.
Boehm, C. (2012). Moral Origins. New York: Basic Books.
Botsman, R. & Rogers, R. (2011). What's Mine Is Yours. London: Collins.
Bottéro, J. (1992). Mesopotamia: Writing, Reasoning And The Gods. Chicago: University of Chicago Press.

Bowlby, J. (1969/1982, 1973, 1980). Attachment and Loss I: Attachment; Attachment and Loss II: Separation, Anxiety and Anger; Loss III: Sadness and Depression. London: Hogarth Press.
Bowles, S., Smith, E. A. & Borgerhof Mulder, M. (2010). Current Anthropology, 51, 7-17. (See also succeeding papers).
Boyd, R. & Richerson, P. (1992). Punishment allows evolution of cooperation (or anything else) in sizeable groups. Ethology and Sociobiology, 13, 171-95.
Boyd, R. & Richerson, P. (2005). The Origin and Evolution of Cultures. Oxford: Oxford University Press.

Cassidy, J. & Shaver, P.R., Eds. (2008). Handbook of Attachment, 2nd Ed.: Theory, Research, and Clinical Applications. New York: Guilford Press.
Chen, X (2011). Culture and children's socioemotional functioning: a contextual-development perspective. In Chen & Rubin (eds.) Socioemotional Development in Cultural Context. New York: Guilford Press.
Chen, X. & Rubin, K., Eds. (2011). Socioemotional Development in Cultural Context. New York: Guilford Press.
Clayton, S.D. & Lerner, M.J. (1991), Complications and complexity in the pursuit of justice. In Hinde, R.A. & Groebel, J. (eds.), Competition and Prosocial Behaviour, pp 173-185. Cambridge: Cambridge University Press.
Colby, A. & Damon, W. (1995). The development of extraordinary moral commitment. In M. Killen & D. Hart (eds). Morality in Everyday Life. Cambridge: Cambridge University Press.

Daly, M. & Wilson, M. (1988). Homicide. New York: Aldine de Gruyter.
Darley, J. & Batson, C.D. (1973). From Jerusalem to Jericho: a study of situational and dispositional variables in helping behavior. J. Pers. Soc. Psychol., 27, 100-08.
Dasgupta, P. (2001). Human Well-Being and the Natural Environment. Oxford: Oxford University Press.
Dasgupta, P. & Ehrlich, P.R. (2013) Pervasive externalities at the population, consumption and environment nexus. Science, 340, 324-327.
Dawkins, R. (1976). The Selfish Gene. Oxford: Oxford University Press.

Dawkins, R. (2006). The God Delusion. London: Transworld.
Dennett, D.C. (1997). Appraising grace: What evolutionary good is God? New York Academy of Sciences, 1997, 53-95.
Des Pres, T. (1976). The Survivor: An Anatomy Of Life In The Death Camps. Oxford University Press: New York.
De Waal, F. (1996). Good Natured. Cambridge: Harvard University Press.
Dormor, D. (2004). Just Cohabiting. London: Darton, Longman & Todd.
Dormor, D. (2008). Science as a moral endeavour. Sermon, St. John's College Cambridge, Nov. 23, 2008.
Drescher, S. (2011). Antislavery debates. European Review, 19, 131-48.
Drewery, J. (1969). An interpersonal perception technique. British J. Medical Psychology, 42, 171-181.
Dunbar, R. (1996). Grooming, Gossip and the Evolution of Language. London: Faber and Faber.

Eagleton, T. (2009). Religion, Faith and Revolution. New Haven CA; Yale University Press.
Edwards, C.P. (2000). Children's play in cross-cultural perspective. Cross-Cultural Research, 34, 318-38.
Eisenberg, N. & Fabes, R.A. (1998). Prosocial development, In W. Damon & N. Eisenberg, (eds.). Handbook of Child Psychology,5th ed., vol.3, pp. 701-778. Wiley: New York.
Ekman, P. (1985). Telling Lies. New York: Norton.
Erdal, D. & Whiten, A. (1996). Egalitarianism and Machiavellian intelligence in human evolution. In Mellars, P. and Gibson, K (eds.), Modelling the Early Human Mind, pp. 139-50. Cambridge: McDonald Institute.
Evans-Pritchard, E. E. (1940). The Nuer. Oxford: Oxford University Press.
Evans-Pritchard, E.E. (1951). Some features of Nuer religion. J. Royal Anthropological Institute, 81, 1-14.

Farsides, T. (2013). The super-altruists. The Psychologist, 26, 734-737.
Farver, J.M., Kim, Y.K. & Lee, Y. (1995). Cultural differences in Korean and Anglo-American preschoolers'social interaction and play behaviours. Child Development, 66, 1088-99.
Fehr, E. & Fischbacher, U. (2003). The nature of human altruism. Nature, 425, 785-91.

Festinger, L. (1957). A Theory of Cognitive Dissonance. Evanston IL: Row Peterson.
Foa, U.G. & E.B. (1974). Societal Structures of the Mind. Springfield Ill: Thomas.
Fredman, R.G. (1981). The Passover Seder. Philadelphia: University of Philadelphia Press.
Frimer, J.A., Walker, J.A. & Dunlop, W.I. (2011). The integration of agency and communion in moral personality. J. Pers. Social Psychology, 101,149-163.

Gomory, R. & Sylla, R. (2013). The American corporation. Daedalus, 142, 102-118.
Graves, N.R. & Graves, T.D. (1983). The cultural context of prosocial development. In D.L.Bridgeman (ed.) The Nature of Prosocial Development. San Diego CA: Academic Press.
Gurven, M. & Winking, J. (2008). Collective action in action: prosocial behaviour in and out of the laboratory. American Anthropology, 110, 179-190.
Guthrie, S. (1993). Faces in the Clouds. New York: Oxford University Press.

Hackney, C.H. & Sanders, G.S. (2003). Religiosity and mental health. J. Scientific Study of Religion, 42, 43-55.
Haidt, J. (2012). The Righteous Mind. London: Allen Lane, Penguin.
Haldane, J.B.S. (1932). The Causes of Evolution. London: Longmans Green.
Hamilton, W.D. (1964). The genetical evolution of social behavior. J. Theoretical Biology, 7, 1-52.
Hannay, D.R. (1980). Religion and health. Social Science and Medicine, 14, 683-85.
Harcourt, A.H. & Stewart, K.J. (2007). Gorilla Society. Chicago: Chicago University Press.
Hardin, G. (1968). The tragedy of the commons. Science, 162, 1243-48.
Harman, O. (2010). The Price of Altruism. London: Bodley Head.
Hauser, M. (2006). Moral Minds. New York: Ecco.
Henrich, J. & Boyd, R. (2001). Why people punish defectors. J. Theoretical Biology, 208, 79-89.
Henrich, J., Boyd, R. & 15 others. (2005). 'Economic Man' in cross-cultural perspective. Behavioral and Brain Sci., 28,795-855.

Hill, K. & Hurtado, M. (1996). Aché life-history: The ecology and demography of a foraging people. Hawthorne NY: Aldine de Gruyter.
Hinde, R.A. (1997). Relationships: A Dialectical Perspective. Hove: Psychology Press.
Hinde, R.A. (1999, 2010). Why Gods Persist. London: Routledge.
Hinde, R.A. (2002). Why Good is Good. London: Routledge.
Hinde, R.A. (2004a). Religious systems. Evolution & Cognition, 10, 3-10.
Hinde, R.A, (2004b). Law and the sources of morality. Phil. Trans.Roy.Soc.B, 359, 1685-95.
Hinde, R.A. (2007). Bending the Rules. Oxford: Oxford University Press.
Hinde, R.A. & Rotblat, J. (2003). War No More. London: Pluto.
Hinde, R.A. & Stevenson-Hinde, J.S. (1973). Constraints on Learning. London: Academic Press.
Hitchens, C. (2007). God is not Great. London: Atlantic.
Hollenbach, D. (2002). The common Good and Christian Ethics. Cambridge: Cambridge University Press.
Holloway, R. (1999). Godless Morality. Edinburgh: Canongate.
Homans, G.C. (1961/1974). Social Behavior: Its Elementary Forms. London: Routledge, Kegan Paul.
Hrdy, S. (1999). Mother Nature. New York: Pantheon.
Hume, D. (1739/1969). A Treatise of Human Nature. London: Penguin.
Hutton, W. (2010). Them and Us. London: Little, Brown.

Irons, W. (1991). How did morality evolve? Zygon, 26, 49-89.

Jacobs, J. (1961). The Death and Life of Great American Cities. London: Vintage.
Jamieson. K. H. (2013). The challenges facing civic education. Daedalus, 2013, 65-83.
Jarrett, C. (2013). The psychology of stuff and things. Psychologist, 26, 560-564.
Johnson, D.D.P. (2005). God's punishment and public goods. Human Nature16, 410-46.
Johnson, P. (1995). The Withered Garland. London: New European Publications.
Kaplan, H. & Hill, K. (1985). Hunting ability and reproductive success among male Aché foragers. Current Anthropology, 26, 131-3.

Kelly, R.L. (1995). The Foraging Spectrum: diversity in hunter-gatherer lifeways. Washington DC: Smithsonian Institution Press.
Krog. A. (1999). Country of My skull. London: Random House.
Küng, H. & Kuschel, L. (1993). A Global Ethic. London: SCM Press.

Lerner, M.J. (1981). The justice motive in human relations. In M.J. & S.C. Lerner, (eds.) The Justice Motive in Social Behaviour. New York: Plenum.
Lewis, M. (1992) Shame. New York: Free Press.

Macfarlane, A. (2008). Japan: Through the Looking Glass. London: Profile Books.
MacLean, C. (1972). Island on the Edge of the World. Edinburgh: Canongate.
McCullough, M.E. (2008). Beyond Revenge. San Francisco CA: Jossey-Bass.
McGuire, W.J. & McGuire, C.V. (1988). Content and process in the experience of self. Advances in Experimental Social Psychology, 21, 97-44.
McKay, R., Efferson, C., Whitehouse, H. & Fehr, E. (2011). Wrath of God: religious primes and punishment. Proc. Roy. Soc. B, 278, 1858-63.
McKay, R. & Whitehouse, H. (in press) Religion and Morality. Psychological Bulletin.
Marlantes, K. (2011). What It Is Like To Go To War. Great Britain: Corvus/ Atlantic.
Martin, M. (1698). A Late Voyage to St. Kilda. London, reprinted Edinburgh: Birlina.
Monroe, K.R. (2010). The Roots of Moral Courage. Cited in Farsides (2013).
Murray, D. (1995). Families in conflict: pervasive violence in Northern Ireland. In Hinde, R.A. & Watson, H. (eds.). War: A Cruel Necessity? London: Tauris.
Murray, S.L. & Holmes, J. G. (1996). The construction of relationship realities. In Fletcher, G. J. O. & Fitness J. (eds.) Knowledge Structures and Interactions in Close Relationships, pp. 911-120. N.J.: Erlbaum.
Nettle, D., Nott, K. & Bateson, M. (2012). 'Cycle thieves: we are watching you'. PLoS ONE 7(12).e51738: doi: 10.1371/journal.pone.0051738.

Norenzayan, A. & Sharif A.F. (2008). The origin and evolution of religious prosociality. Science, 322, 58-62.
Norenzayan, A., Smith, E.E., Kim, B.J. & Nisbett, R.E. (2002). Cultural preferences for formal versus intuitive reasoning. Cognitive Science, 26, 653-84.
Nowak, M.A. & Sigmund, K. (1998) The dynamics of indirect reciprocity. J. theoretical Biology, 194, 561-574.
Nowak, M.A. & Sigmund, K. (2005). Evolution of indirect reciprocity. Nature, 437, 1291-1298.
Nucci, L. & Lee, J. (1993). Morality and personal autonomy. In G.G.Noam & T.E.Wran (eds). The Moral Self. Cambridge MA: MIT Press.

O'Keefe, J. (1996). I'll tell you a secret. An introduction to Catholic social teaching. Catholic Agency for Overseas Development.

Parkes, C. M., Stevenson-Hinde, J., & Marris, P. (eds.) (1991). Attachment across the Life Cycle. London: Routledge.
Petrinovich, L.(1995). Human Evolution. New York: Plenum.
Picketty, T. (2014). Capital in the Twenty-first Century. Cambridge, Mass: Harvard University Pres.
Prins, K.S., Buunk. B.P. & Van Yperen,N.W. (1993). Equity, normative disapproval and extramarital relationships. J. Social and Personal Relationships, 10, 39-53.
Putnam, R. (2000). Bowling Alone: The Collapse and Revival of American Community. Cambridge, Mass: Harvard University Press.

Roemer, J.E. (1996). Egalitarian Perspectives. Cambridge: Cambridge University Press.

Sainsbury, D. (2013). Progressive capitalism: How to Achieve Economic Growth, Liberty, and Social Justice. London: Biteback Publishing.
Sands, P. (2008). Torture Team: Deception, Cruelty and the Compromise of Law. London: Allen Lane.
Santos, M. dos, Rankin, D.J. & Wedkind, C. (2011). The evolution of punishment through reputation. Proc. Roy Soc. B., 278, 371-377.
Scheper-Hughes, N. (1992). Death without Weeping: The Violence of Everyday Life in Brazil. Berkeley, CA: University of California Press.

Seligman, M.E.P & Hager, J.L. (1972). Biological Boundaries of Learning, New York: Appleton Century Crofts.
Seyfarth, R.M.& Cheney, D. (2012). The evolutionary origins of friendship. Annual Review of Psychology, 63, 4.1 – 4,25.
Sharif, A.F. & Norenzayan, A. (2007). God is watching you: priming god concepts in an anonymous economic game. Psychological Science, 18, 803-09.
Shor, E. & Roelfs, D.J. (2013). The longevity effects of religious and non-religious participation: A meta-analysis and meta-regression. Sci. Study of Religion.52,120-145.
Shweder R.A. & Bourne, E. (1984). Does the concept of the person vary cross-culturally? In Culture theory. R. Shweder & R. LeVine, (eds.) pp. 158-99. Cambridge: Cambridge University Press.
Shweder, R.A., Mahapatra, M. & Miller, J.G. (1990). Culture and moral development. In Stigler et al., (eds), Cultural Psychology. Cambridge: Cambridge University Press
Stevenson-Hinde, J. (2011). Culture and socio-emotional development, with a focus on fearfulness and attachment. In Chen & Rubin (eds.), Socioemotional Development in Cultural Context (pp. 11-28). New York: Guilford Press.
Stiglitz, J. (2006). Making Globalization Work. London: Penguin.
Szreter, S. (2005). Health by association? Social capital, social theory and the public economy of public health. In S. Szreter (ed.), Health and Wealth. Rochester NY: University of Rochester Press.
Szreter, S, (2010). The WHO and the Social Determinants of Health Report 2008. In S. Bhattacharya, S. Messenger & C. Overy (eds.) Social Determinants of Health. Hyderabad: Orint Black Swan.

Thorpe, W.H. (1961). Bird song. Cambridge: Cambridge University Press.
Toynbee, P. & Walker, D. (2008). Unjust Rewards. London: Granta.
Triandis, H.C. (1991). Cross-cultural differences in assertiveness/ competitiveness vs group loyalty/cooperation. In R.A.Hinde & J. Groebel (eds.), Cooperation and Prosocial Behaviour. Cambridge: Cambridge University Press.
Trivers, R. (1974). Parent–infant conflict. American Zoologist,14, 249-64.
Trivers, R. (1985). Social Evolution. Menlo Park CA: Benjamin/ Cummings.
van IJzendoorn, M.H. & Sagi, A. (2008). Cross-cultural patterns of attachment: Universal and contextual dimensions. In J. Cassidy & P.

Shaver (eds.). Handbook of Attachment, 2nd Ed.: Theory, Research, and Clinical Applications. New York: Guilford Press.

Walster, E., Walster, G.W. & Berscheid E. (1978). Equity Theory and Research. Boston, MA: Allyn & Bacon.

Warneken, T. (2013). Young children proactively remedy unnoticed accidents. Cognition, 126, 101-108.

Wareneken, T. & Tomasello, M. (2009). The roots of human altruism. British Journal of Psychology, 100, 455-471.

Warnock, M. (2004). An Intelligent Person's Guide to Ethics. London: Duckworth.

Whitehouse, H. (2000). Arguments and Icons: Divergent Modes of Religiosity. Oxford: Oxford University Press.

Whiten, A. (1994). On human egalitarianism: An evolutionary product of Machiavellian status escalation? Current Anthropology, 35, 175-183.

Wiessner, P. (2002). Hunting, healing, and *hxaro* exchange: A long-term perspective on !Kung (Ju/'hoansi) large-game hunting. Evolution and Human Behaviour, 23, 407-436.

Wilkinson, R. & Pickett, K. (2009). The Spirit Level. London: Penguin.

Williams, B. (1985). Ethics and the Limits of Philosophy. London: Fontana.

Williams, G.C. (1966). Adaptation and Natural Selection. Princeton NJ: Princeton University Press.

Wilson, D.S., (2002). Darwin's Cathedral: Evolution, Religion and the Nature of Society. Chicago Ill: University of Chicago Press.

Wrangham, R.W., Wilson, M.L. & Muller, M.N. (2006). Comparative rates of aggression in chimpanzees and humans. Primates, 47, 14-26.

# Index

Attachment  92, 93, 95-96
Authoritarianism  68-69

Belief and morality  47-50
Biased views  56, 58
Blitz  13

Capitalism  74-76, 78-83
Carrot & stick  62-63, 95
Celebrity culture  16-17
CEO's responsibilities  75-76
Chimpanzee  35, 40
Churches & morality  87
Climate change 77
Cohousing  101
Communal good  14, 101
Competition  73-77, 83
Competitive games  73
Conflict  17-18, 35, 42, 57, 105; inter-group 42-43
Conscience  45, 49-50
Consumerism  79
Criteria  66-67
Cultural change  22, 27, 55, 58-60, 68, 117-119
Cultural differences  106-107

Despair  19
Development of behaviour  32-33, 61, 91
Dialectical relations  24-27, 59, 61
Disasters  13-14
Divorce  26-27
Duelling  116

Education  95-97
'Egalitarian societies'  40-42, 108-112,

Employee ownership  83-84
Empowerment of women  95
Environmental change  65, 73
Exchange theories  38-40

Fairness  21, 38-40, 74, 107-108
Foot-binding  116-117
Forgiving  36

Goals  56, 94-95
Golden Rule  34, 38, 65, 74
Gossip  41, 62, 108-109, 112
Greed  17, 19, 31

Honour  116-117
Human rights & responsibilities  97-100
Humanism  68
Humility  79

Individual responsibility 55, 59, 86
Individualism & collectivism  100-102
Inequalities  78-79
Infanticide  51-66
In-group vs. out-group  45-46
Institutions 71, 73-89, 105
Integrity Action  118-119
Intention  66
Intentional communities  101
Intuition or rational debate  50-52

Japanese characteristics & culture  19, 112-115

Law  57
Leaders  109
Limited change  56

Lobbying 85

Machiavellian societies 41-42
Marketplace 74-78
Materialism 56-57, 79
Media 14, 19, 79
Multi-disciplinary approach 20
Mutual understanding 92-93

Nepotism 37-38, 56

Optimism 19
Original sin 67

Paedophilia 64
Parental care 37-38, 90, 96
Personal freedom 65, 90, 99-100, 109
Personal relationships 92-95
Politics 85-87
Population 90-91
Poverty 61, 81-82, 97
Prisoners 99
Prosocial propensities 14-15, 19, 21
Prosociality & selfish assertiveness 14-18, 59, 101, 105
Punishment 36, 38, 40, 43-44, 95, 109

Reciprocity 38
Religious schools 36-37, 97

Religious tolerance 59, 97
Reproductive biology 64, 95
Revenge 35-36
Rewards & punishment 62-63
Rules & values 65

Sanpo Yoshi 115
Science & morality 19-24
Self-assertiveness 94
Self-concept 49, 58
Sharing 110, 115
Slavery 20, 63-64, 117
Social capital 86, 95, 101-102
Societal values 64
Society today 13-18

Terrorists 99
Theory of mind 93
Tsunami 13, 19, 114-115

Urban living 91-92

Values 24, 51, 65, 95-97

War & morality 20, 87-89
Wealth-gap 15, 17, 61, 65, 78-80, 105
Whistle blowers 112
Women, empowerment of 97
World-view 15, 18, 20, 23, 59, 61-62, 91, 105